Low Cholesterol Diet Recipes

Living Healthy with Smoothie Diet and Kale Recipes

Lisa Graham

Table of Contents

VEGETABLE SMOOTHIES (ALSO KNOWN AS GREEN SMOOTHIES) 161

Low Cholesterol Diet Recipes Introduction

Kale, the Mother of all Super Foods for Low Cholesterol Diets

Find much more than recipes in this fact filled book that provides a no-fuss way to begin a low cholesterol diet. You will learn what foods make a positive difference in your life, and provide reasons why certain foods affect your weight and health, in negative ways. Be the first to share the Mother of all Super Foods with family and friends that include unique recipes for morning, noon, and night.

The secret is out on how Super Food, Kale, is stepping up to center plate, saying, 'move over berries, bananas and celery'. Actually, these neighbors run a close second to the nutritional value of kale, but this leafy little veggie has been kept quiet for way too long. Cholesterol lowering, fat, burning, known for improving mental clarity and heavy in antioxidants, it was only a matter of time before someone came up with a complete cookbook of low cholesterol diet recipes, with kale as the ingredient.

The first part of this book explains how kale has been examined, how it is grown, the nutritional properties, and how it has been hailed as being a cancer preventative food. Next, get prepared for the recipes that will amaze and delight you. Ten breakfast recipes that include kale, eggs, feta cheese, burritos, quiche, muffins, and yummy green smoothies, gives you a sneak preview of what lies ahead.

Protein-rich kale soups, ten in all, packed full of vitamins A, C, and K, are presented chilled and hot, spicy or hearty, and come highly recommended for improving the cardiovascular system. If you are a salad person, welcome to kale. Ten lunch choices, with fresh ingredients, that may seem a little unusual for salads, will become a regular on your daily meal planner. Avocado, apricots, watermelon, radish, lemon, oranges, Parmesan, and tofu, are a few of the different flavors that are mixed, expertly, with herbs and seasonings.

Main dishes prove to be just as appealing, with Cajun chicken, scallion fried rice, lasagna, and steamed halibut with walnuts, for examples of how low cholesterol meals do not have to be boring and bland. Kale is included in all of these recipes, blended in uniquely so several flavors are present, and the vitamins, an added surprise. Here comes the best part, delicious, easy to make desserts that are only second to heaven. Try the Coconut and Chocolate Kale Chips that have cashews, cinnamon, maple syrup, cocoa, coconut flakes, vanilla, and of course, kale, for a treat that will amaze your guests. It's up to you, whether or not, to share this secret recipe.

Kale belongs to the same family as broccoli, Brussels sprouts and cabbage, but you have probably seen it as a garnishment alongside a main dish and never thought twice about it. It has 192% of the recommended daily allowance of vitamin A in a single serving and 90% of the recommended daily allowance of vitamin C in a one cup serving. You cannot overdose on too much vitamin A and C. In fact, you will probably just replace the amount that preservatives have stolen. Also known to be a 'bad' cholesterol blocker, you will wonder where this extreme food has been hiding all of your life.

The second part of this book gets even better with Smoothies. Smoothies are all the craze these days, but only if they are prepared correctly. Using packaged drink mixes and sugar-laden fruit juice, may give you the opinion that you are drinking healthy, but look at the labels. Toss this stuff out that contributes to fat around the waist and destroys precious antioxidants that your body works so hard to produce. Start from scratch with a blender. Make sure you use a really sturdy blender, or use a separate ice crusher. You may select to add a juicer to your small appliances for removing pulp, but many like the rich texture and make it thick enough to eat with a spoon.

There is a wide variety of smoothies that start with fruit, vegetables, or tofu and make a scrumptious treat, drink, or meal, depending on how you make them. Beware, everything that is used in these smoothies, is vitamin-rich, delicious and low cholesterol. You may want to freeze certain fruits and vegetables so you can enjoy your favorite drinks after the growing season is past.

A section on how to care for your kale is included. Once you discover this inexpensive bundle of health, you will want to keep plenty on hand. Every part of the kale, except the stem, can be consumed and keeping it fresh, is important. Tips, like what to look for when buying the freshest kale, how to wash and the best way to store, are also shared.

Almost any flavor of smoothie that you can imagine, is spelled out simply, and made for one serving. This can be increased if you are serving others. Green smoothies may be something that you have never tried but will soon fall in love with. Comparable to the chilled soups, they are tasty, thick and thirst quenching. The Veggie Nut is very popular, combining veggies, fruits and nuts in a reunion of taste, and will soon become your favorite, too.

As an added feature, there is a 5-day sample menu if you are ready for a weight loss program. After sampling everything on this handy menu, create your own mixtures from the menus included. Keep active, exercising regularly. You will find that your energy level is improved and your mental clarity, becoming sharper. There has never been a better time to get those extra pounds off and to begin a nutritional program for the whole family. The best part is, they will never know that they are eating healthy. It can be your little secret.

Section 1: All About Kale: Why is it a Superfood?

There are many foods that are good for the body. Fruits and vegetables are considered to be part of a healthy diet. There are some foods that are known as super foods. They contain a number of vitamins and minerals. In addition to promoting good health they can help with ailments as well. Kale is considered to be one of these super foods. Usually, kale is simply used as a garnish, or thrown in with other collard greens. But, as you'll discover throughout this book, there are far more uses than that.

Kale is a vegetable with a high number of nutrients. It is one of the healthiest foods that a person can eat. Kale is in the same vegetable family as broccoli, cabbage, and Brussels sprouts. it is packed with more vitamins per bite than many other vegetables. This vegetable will help keep a person healthy. Kale can even help the body defend itself against cancer. This food can help prevent stomach, colon, breast, and ovarian cancers.

Kale is able to help the body stay healthy by providing the daily values of many different vitamins. Kale is high in vitamin K, vitamin A, and vitamin C. It also contains a significant amount of copper and manganese. Kale has an adequate amount of many other vitamins including vitamin B6, potassium, calcium, thiamin, riboflavin, niacin, zinc, and iron. Kale also contains omega 3 fatty acids which help with memory and brain development.

Kale has many anti-oxidant powers that will keep a person from getting ill, and can help fight off any pre existing illness. Some of the anti-oxidants that can be found in kale include B-carotene, lutein, and zeaxanthin. The carotene will help a person keep their eyes strong and healthy. This vitamin is also said to improve the vision of a person that is having trouble seeing already. One study found that people who ate a lot of kale in their diet were able to reduce their risk of developing cataracts by fifty percent.

Kale is low in calories and these calories are easy for the body to use and to burn. A one cup serving of kale has only 36 calories. This same serving size has 192% of a person's recommended daily amount of Vitamin A. It is said that the body cannot overdose on vitamin A. This same serving of kale is around 90% of the daily value of vitamin C that is recommended for a person to stay healthy. Vitamin C will help prevent cells from being damaged and will help the body repair any cells that are damaged. This vitamin will also help inflammation and help to keep cholesterol at a healthy level. Vitamin C will also help the body fight off colds and other illnesses.

Kale contains trace minerals that help with certain functions of the body. Manganese will help the body burn and use different types of fatty acids. They will also help the acid reach sex cells and the nervous system for use. These minerals will also aid the body in using and burning both proteins and carbohydrates. Kale can help the body burn fat and keep the body for storing new fatty deposits. The amount of calcium that is found in kale will help the body to keep strong bones. It will also help to prevent the onset of osteoporosis. This mineral will also promote the development of collagen in the skin, which will help a person remain youthful in appearance.

Kale is one of the three green and leafy vegetables that can keep a person mentally sharp even as they age. This vegetable will slow the mental decline in a person that comes with old age. Kale alone can slow this mental decline down by 40%. This is similar to reversing the aging process by five years. Kale has many vitamins and minerals that benefit the inside of the body as well. Kale contains a photochemical known as idole-3-carbinol. This biochemical will help lower the amount of secretion from the liver. It also blocks the transfer of the LDL also known as the "bad cholesterol" from entering the tissues in the body and getting into the blood stream. Kale will also help a person burn stubborn belly fat that exercise and diet alone do not get rid of.

With all of these nutrients and vitamins in kale it is a natural fat burner. It is very low in calories and does not contain fat. Kale will help the body with its urinary track systems as well. Kale helps to protect the bladder as well as bladder cancer. Many people that have had urinary tract infections know how painful this can be. Eating kale can help a person from getting this condition. This one again is due to the amount of vitamin A that is found in this leafy vegetable.

In order to get the most health benefits out of kale it should be eaten soon after being purchased. Kale can also be grown in a garden. Kale has a rating of 1,770 on the ORAC scale. This scale is a rating of the amount of antioxidants that are found in food. Other vegetables only have ratings that are in the hundreds. Kale has a rating of at least a thousand more than other vegetables on this scale.

While kale is good for the body it is not the most attractive vegetable to eat. Kale is dark green in color and curly. There are several ways that a person can prepare kale. It can be chopped up while it is raw and added to salads. It can be cooked and included in casseroles, soups, and stir fries. With all the benefits to the body this super food contains, it does not matter how a person eats it. Many of the recipes that contain kale are low in calories and low in fat. Kale provides so many vitamins and minerals, it could be eaten on a daily basis to help a person stay healthy.

How to Store Kale

Kale is the buzz word among busy families looking for an easy to prepare, nutrient-dense food. Kale offers variety from other leafy greens. Whether choosing the younger, tender leaves for intense, flavorful salads, or the more mature leaves for cooking as a side dish of wilted greens, kale is finding a place on more and more tables. As this super food becomes more widely known, people everywhere are asking how to choose it, how to use it, and how best to keep it on hand to enjoy any time.

Kale is a deep green leafy member of the cruciferous family, a relative of broccoli, collards, cabbage, and Brussels sprouts. It is available in several varieties, including curly, the most common, ornamental, and Tuscan, with its longer, more slender leaves.

As with any fresh produce, there are a number of things to consider when choosing Kale at the market for flavor, freshness and optimum storage. First, consider how you will serve it. Larger leaves may be bitter for salads, but will cook well to serve as a side dish of greens. Younger more tender leaves are ideal for salads. Look for strong stems, not limp.

The firm leaves should be a deep green. Avoid signs of yellow or brown leaves or small holes in the leaves. Avoid signs of wilting, which indicate an older product that probably will not store well, and may be more likely to contain contaminants. In fact, you may want to consider choosing an organically raised product, as Kale is a member of the most widely contaminated produce varieties known as "the dirty dozen."

However, it's delicious and nutritious benefits far outweigh any risks, and you should not hesitate to make kale a new and permanent part of your family's diet. Proper preparation and storage is the key. In general, kale can be prepared for storage just as one would prepare it for serving. Whether for use as a salad green or for cooking, it is best to remove the tough stems.

Grab the stem firmly in one hand and with a tight grip of the other hand, pull down and away, stripping the tender leaves from the stem. The leaves themselves will stay fairly well intact. Toss the stems away, and toss the leaves into a cold water bath. Agitate the leaves to remove any grit and soil. Remove the leaves, squeezing out any excess water. From here you can choose to boil the kale and serve it wilted as a side dish, serve it fresh in a salad, or store it to enjoy later.

To store it you may refrigerate it or freeze it. If you are refrigerating, it is very important at this point to get the kale as dry as possible. For this reason, many people prefer to refrigerate it without washing, and clean it as they use it. If you wash it first, blot it as dry as possible with paper towels. Place the kale in sealable plastic bags, removing as much of the air as possible as you seal it. In the coldest part of the refrigerator, it should keep well for 5 to 7 days. Be aware that the leaves will become more bitter, the longer kale is kept. For longer storage, kale can also be frozen. Clean and wash it as described above. Blanch the leaves for 2 minutes in boiling water, and plunge them immediately into an ice water bath. Drain and place the blanched kale in sealable freezer bags, removing as much of the air as possible. Kale can be kept frozen for 10 to 12 months. One advantage of freezing is that frozen kale can tend to have a slightly sweeter taste, not as bitter as fresh.

If kale becomes a regular part of your family's diet, as it has for many, consider growing it yourself. Let nature herself handle the storage for you. The leaves can be harvested for each intended use, young tender leaves for salads, older leaves to be cooked. Just pick as needed and the kale keeps producing so that you can harvest as you go, just as you would with cut and come again lettuces. Kale is a hardy winter vegetable. Frost actually improves its flavor. And you can store it frozen right in the garden to enjoy all winter long. Mature plants will survive right through the toughest winter weather, down to 10°F or below.

Finally, one of the most popular uses for kale lately is in the form of bite-size dehydrated chips. Kale chips are available in health food markets everywhere. They don't stay on the shelves long, and they won't stay in the house long once your family has tasted this trendy new snack. But healthy as they are, delicious kale chips can be expensive. Consider making them yourself at home. There are many easy recipes readily available online, but here is perhaps the simplest. Just tear tender young kale leaves into bite-size pieces, coat in extra-virgin olive oil and sea salt, and spread them out on rimmed baking sheets.

Without an expensive food dehydrator, you can roast them for an hour in a very low oven, 170°F. Turn off the heat and let them rest in the oven another half hour. Then turn the oven back on for another 20 minutes. The result will be crispy delicious salty chips your family or party guests will rave about. Leftover chips will keep well for several days in a brown paper bag. If they become soft, they can be re-crisped in a low oven and served again as fresh as just-made.

Kale is a super food which is growing in popularity. It is easy to find and easy to keep on hand. Whether you enjoy it as a salad, as wilted greens, or as a substitute for your favorite salty snack chip, whether you shop for it at the local market or grow it yourself, you can make kale a delicious new choice for your family's table.

10 Great Kale Recipes: Breakfast

Easy Breakfast Casserole

Ingredients

8 eggs
1/2 cup chopped ham, sausage or bacon bits
1/4 teaspoon salt
1 cup fresh kale, finely chopped
Pinch black pepper
1 cup shredded cheese (white cheddar)
1/4 cup Parmesan cheese
1/2 cup half and half
3 or 4 chopped scallions
Directions
Preheat oven to 350°
Prepare a 9 x 13 inch casserole dish with non-stick cooking spray.

Beat together the black pepper, salt, half and half and eggs.

Mix in kale.

Add ham, sausage or bacon.

Pour the ingredients the casserole dish.

Top casserole with Cheddar and Parmesan cheeses then garnish with chopped scallions.

Bake 30-40 minutes, or until the middle is firm.

Breakfast Burrito

Ingredients

4 large eggs
2 7 ½ inch flour tortillas
2 tablespoons milk
1 tablespoon fresh cilantro (chopped)
1/2 cup fresh chopped kale
2 tablespoons olive oil
1/2 cup grated Pepper Jack or Monterey Jack
Pepper and Salt
2 tablespoons sour cream (optional)

Directions

Preheat the oven to 350°F then place the tortillas in foil, wrap them and place them in oven to warm.

Whisk the pepper, salt, milk, cilantro and eggs in a bowl.

Add olive oil to a skillet (nonstick) over medium-low heat.

Add kale, stirring for about 1 minute then put in eggs and cook, while stirring, until just firm. Spoon eggs along the middle of the tortillas then top with sour cream and cheese. Fold tortilla.

Kale Omelet with Mushrooms and Feta Cheese

Ingredients

Pepper and Salt
1 tablespoon feta cheese
1 teaspoon olive oil
1/4 cup mushroom pieces (fresh)
1 cup fresh kale
2 eggs (beaten)

Directions

Heat oil in a small skillet on med heat then put in mushrooms and kale and sauté until the mushrooms are properly heated and the kale starts to wilt.

Put in eggs. Cook until eggs are firm, lifting the edges to let uncooked part of egg flow to the bottom. Flip if desired.

Add pepper and salt to taste.

Put in feta cheese then, fold in half and serve.

Super Green Smoothie

Ingredients

1 cup fresh kale
1 tablespoon lemon juice
1/4 cup orange juice or water
1/2 cup fresh blueberries
1 banana
4 ice cubes

Directions

Blend together the water/orange juice, blueberries, banana and ice cubes until consistency is smooth. Put in kale and blend again until completely smooth and creamy.

Wilted Kale

Ingredients

1 cup sliced mushrooms
2 cups kale
1 lb bacon

Directions

Fry bacon then put to one side
Put mushrooms and kale in bacon grease then stir over
medium-high heat until well-heated and kale starts to
wilt.

Serve immediately.

Ham and Cheese Pinwheels

Ingredients:

1 packet ranch dressing mix (dry)
4 oz sour cream
4 oz spreadable whipped cream cheese
Fresh kale leaves
4-8 slices deli ham (or turkey ham)
1 can crescent rolls

Directions

Grease cookie sheet. Preheat oven to 400. Then roll the crescent rolls out.

In a bowl, whisk together ranch dressing mix, cream cheese and sour cream.

Spread mixture in a thin layer over the crescents.

Add one slice of ham and one kale leaf to each crescent.

Roll lengthwise then to close the dough pinch the ends.

Bake until golden brown (15-20 minutes).

Let cool for 10 minutes then Cut into bite-sized slices.

Breakfast Pizza Casserole

Ingredients

1 cup grated Cheddar cheese
6 eggs
1/2 cup chopped onion
2 cups shredded kale
1 cup frozen hash brown potatoes (thaw)
1 can crescent dinner rolls
1 lb. ground pork sausage

Directions

Brown sausage in a skillet, then let drain and put to one side.

Unroll the crescent roll into a baking dish that is lightly greased. Press the sides and bottom to make a crust. Use a fork to create several small holes.

Bake crust at 350 degrees on the lower rack in the oven for 5 - 6 minutes. Spoon the over crust evenly then top with kale, onion and potatoes.

Beat eggs and pour mixture over potatoes then bake without covering dish at 350 degrees on until set (approximately 25 minutes) on lower oven rack.

Sprinkle cheese evenly over top then let bake until cheese melts (approximately 5 minutes).

Kale Quiche

Ingredients

Dash black pepper
1/2 tsp. salt
3 slices crumbled cooked bacon
2 beaten eggs
1 cup milk
2 cups cooked kale
2 tablespoons flour
2 cups shredded cheese (sharp cheddar)
1 ready-to-use pie crust (refrigerated)

Directions

Preheat oven to 350°F.

Place crust in a pie plate (9-inch) then flute edge and use a fork to prick.

In medium sized bowl mix flour and cheese then put in remaining ingredients. Pour mixture into crust and let bake for approximately 1 hour.

Kale Cake Muffins

Ingredients

1 1/2 cups flour (all purpose)
1/2 cup unsweetened applesauce
2 tablespoons oil (vegetable)
1 teaspoon powder (baking)
1/3 cup sugar
1 cup fresh kale
2 teaspoons vanilla extract
1/2 teaspoon baking soda
1 large egg
1/2 teaspoon salt

Directions

Preheat the oven to 350 F.

Use a food processor to puree oil, sugar, kale, vanilla, egg and applesauce.

In another bowl mix the dry ingredients.

Pour the puree into a big mixing bow then slowly mix in dry ingredients until well combined.

Place batter in lined or greased mini muffin tin (only fill two thirds of each cup).

Bake 12-15 minutes.

English Muffin Personal Pizzas

Ingredients

1 teaspoon salt
Oregano
Mozzarella (grated)
1/2 cup kale (finely chopped)
2 sliced hard-cooked eggs
Slices of tomato
4 teaspoons olive oil
4 English muffins

Directions

Cut English muffins in half and toast them then place them on a cookie sheet.

Drizzle the olive oil on each one.

Place one slice of tomato on each half of muffin.

Layer on 2 or 3 egg slices

Add desired amount of cheese then garnish with lots of kale.

Add salt and oregano

Broil for approximately 5 minutes (until cheese melts).

10 Great Kale Recipes: Soup

The dark leafy green vegetable is making fine cuisine taste even better. Kale is a Superfood packed with vitamins and fiber. Improve your health and your appearance with Kale Soup Recipes.

A one cup serving of kale contains RDA recommended nutrients:

2.5 g Protein
354% Vitamin A (beta-carotene)
89% Vitamin C
1328% Vitamin K
27% Manganese

Protect your cardio vascular system from heart disease. Also identified as a cancer fighting agent, Kale induces blood and bone regeneration. Balance your body with Kale Superfood Soups to beat chronic ailments. Kale assists the body in absorption of Calcium and Magnesium required for longevity. Ten (10) Delicious Kale Superfood Soup recipes can be prepared raw or cooked.

Kale Gazpacho

Summer Soup in Minutes

Ingredients

1 kale bun
1t olive oil
2 garlic cloves
1t salt

Directions

Toss cooked kale into a blender, add a little olive oil and salt, garlic and let chill. Add a lemon or lime for a fresh summer soup first or main course. Pour over BBQ meats. Kale Gazpacho is also great with cut vegetables or warm bread.

Dilled Kale, Beets and Tofu Soup

Rich Winter Soup

Ingredients

1 kale bun
1 bunch/can of beets
1 box of tofu
1 garlic clove
1t wine vinegar
Salt

Directions

Heat the olive oil in a frying pan over medium high heat. The beets and tofu should be browned before turning the heat down. When tender, add the kale, garlic, wine vinegar, and salt and cook for to a bright green consistency.

Cool. Add the mixture to the blender.

In the winter the soup can be poured as gravy over mashed potatoes. Add 2T of olive oil, 2T of fresh dill chopped, and salt to taste.

Kale and Bean Soup

A Whole Meal

Ingredients

1 canned or fresh cooked white beans
1 kale bun
1t olive oil
Salt

Directions

Heat the olive oil in a frying pan over medium high heat.
Add beans. Simmer. Turn down the heat and add the
kale. When tender, add salt and hot sauce.

Sri Lanka Kale Coconut Soup

Southeast Asian Flavor

Ingredients

1 chopped red onion
1 to 2 chopped hot chili peppers (remove seeds)
12 oz of thinly sliced kale (remove stems)
1/4 tsp ground cumin
1/2 cup shredded coconut, fresh or frozen
1 to 2 t of lime juice
Ground pepper
Salt to taste

Directions

Heat a large non-stick skillet and add the chopped
onions and peppers. Simmer. Add water sparingly to
avoid sticking. Once hot, add the kale and a 1/4 cup of
water, followed by the cumin and pepper seasoning. Stir
cooking for 4 to 5 minutes until the kale is wilted. Only
add water if more soup is desired. Finally, add the
coconut and 1 T of lime juice. Turn off the heat, salt to
taste. Serve hot or cold. Total preparation time: 10
minutes.

Sesame Noodle & Kale Soup

A Taste of the Orient

Ingredients

1 large bunch kale
3 teaspoons soy sauce
2 tablespoons sesame seeds
1 teaspoon brown sugar
1 teaspoon vinegar (rice wine)

Directions

Wash bunch of Kale, removing the thicker stems then cut the Kale into ribbons 1 cm long, place in a strainer and set aside. Sprinkle with 1T of salt and rub salt into the stalks.

In a small frying pan, toast the sesame seeds until golden brown over low heat. Add Kale and simmer. Cool and mix with the soy sauce, wine vinegar and brown sugar in a food processor or blender. Add water and reheat to boil. Add noodles. Salt the soup to taste.

Tuscan Kale Soup

A Taste of Italy

Ingredients

1 bun of kale
2t olive oil
2 cloves of garlic
1 box bowtie pasta
1 handful of rock salt

Directions

Heat olive oil, salt and garlic in a sauce pan. Add washed and cut kale to the oil. Simmer until limp. Remove from heat. Boil water, add rock salt. Cook bowtie pasta. Drain the pasta and add it to the kale mixture. Add ¼ cup of water and slightly boil.

Kale & Avocado Gazpacho

Green Goddess Raw Soup for the Soul

Ingredients

1 kale bun shredded
1 cup tomato chopped
1/2 avocado
1-2 t olive oil or hemp seed oil
1/2 lemon
Sea salt, to taste
1/8 tsp cayenne

Directions

Add olive oil to saucepan. Toss in salt while heating. Add kale and 1T of water. Cool. Add kale to blender with the remainder of the ingredients.

Serve with lemon.

Raw Kale Soup

A True Raw Concoction- Boost with Protein Powder

Ingredients

1 kale bun shredded
1 carrot
2t olive or sesame oil
2 garlic cloves
Salt
Protein powder (optional)

Directions

Blend shredded kale and carrot. Add olive oil, garlic and salt. Flavorless protein powder will enhance the power of your superfood soup. Drink up.

Sesame Kale Soup

An Oshitashi, Steamed Japanese Dish

Ingredients

1 kale bun
12 oz. soba, udon, fettuccine or spaghetti
2 t sesame oil (toasted) or additional for taste
2 t tamari or additional to taste
2 t black or white sesame seeds (toasted)

Directions

Place sliced kale into a pot of boiling water. Remove and wash again. Let water come to a boil once more then out in pasta and let cook until al dente. Add kale and cook uncovered over high heat. Drain pasta and kale and return to pot with sesame oil and tamari. Add sesame seeds and serve hot.

Green Power Soup

Kale and Broccoli Paired Up for Optimum Blood
Efficiency

Ingredients

1 kale bun
1-2 large broccoli florets
2 t toasted sesame oil or to taste
2 t tamari or to taste
2 t toasted white or black sesame seeds

Directions

Place sliced broccoli and kale into a pot of salted boiling
water then cook until wilted. Remove and cool. Place
the greens in a food processor or blender with the
sesame oil and tamari. Heat up or serve cold. Sprinkle
sesame seeds on top.

10 Great Kale Recipes: Salads

Everyone knows that Kale is one of the best greens your body can consume. So why not use it as a replacement for other green dishes. Let's replace the romaine lettuce with fresh kale in our raw salads. The great thing about salads is that they are quick, easy, and convenient. Everybody loves something that they can throw together on the go. Kale can be a bit chewy so before you make a raw kale salad, considered massaging it a bit to soften it up, then enjoy. Here are a few great Kale salad ideas that your friends, family, and yourself can enjoy and make.

Kale Salad with Parmesan, Avocado and Apricots

Keep in mind this is a serving size for one, you can always add or remove any ingredients as preferred. Also add more for groups.

Ingredients

1/2 avocado
2 tablespoons vinegar (red wine)
1 tablespoon olive oil (extra-virgin)
8-10 flakes of cheese (Parmesan)
1/4 cup almonds
1/3 cup cooked beans
6-8 apricots (dried)
6-8 ounces of kale
Pepper and salt

Directions

Once you have your Kale go ahead and use tear into pieces using fingers. Remember to rip off the middle hard part of the kale. Make sure you tear them into bite size pieces and place into a medium size bowl.

Cut the apricots up into tiny pieces and put them in the

bowl. Also throw in your beans, almonds, and cheese. Stir together your vinegar and oil, and pour all over with a dash of salt.

Cube the avocados and put them all over salad. The salad can stay fresh for twenty-four hours.

Tuscan Kale Salad

This salad keeps it very simple. This is the ultimate raw kale salad. All you need to do is tear up your kale and throw it in a bowl. Put whatever dressing you would like over it but here is a recipe for a great Tuscan flavorful dressing.

Ingredients

Parmesan or Pecorino Cheese
Garlic
Red pepper flakes
Pepper and salt
Lemon juice
Olive oil

Directions

Mix altogether and let it sit on the kale for about 10-15 minutes, then serve.

Pickled Watermelon Radish with Kale Salad

Ingredients

1/4 cup toasted pumpkin seeds
Black pepper (freshly ground)
1 teaspoon thyme leaves (fresh)
1 teaspoon lemon juice
1 tablespoon pumpkin seed oil (toasted)
2 tablespoons olive oil (extra virgin)
1 bunch kale
1 watermelon radish (regular radishes can be used)
Kosher salt
1/4 cup sugar
1/2 cup vinegar (white wine)

Directions

Combined salt, sugar and vinegar in a medium size bowl.
Slice the radish thinly and add to the bowl. Stir
everything together to make sure that the radish slices
are fully saturated. Let it stand for about 30 minutes.

Tear kale into bite size pieces. In a large bowl mix all
other ingredients - thyme, lemon juice, pumpkin seed oil
and olive oil. Add the kale into the bowl and massage
together. Drain the radishes and toss into the large

bowl. Use pumpkin seeds to garnish.

Kale Salad with Lemon and Pecorino

Ingredients

Fresh black pepper and Kosher salt (to taste)
1/2 cup olive oil
2 juiced lemons
4 ounces grated Pecorino Romano
1 big bunch kale washed and trim the stems off

Directions

Cut the kale into ribbon length pieces. Toss the cheese together with kale. Stir together lemon juice and olive oil and pour over the salad. Season with salt and pepper then let stand for about an hour prior to serving.

Kale Salad with Meyer Lemon and Blood Orange

Ingredients

Freshly ground black pepper and kosher salt
1/4 cup olive oil (extra-virgin)
1 large finely chopped shallot
Zest of 1 Meyer lemon
4 small segmented blood oranges (reserve the juice)
1 bunch black kale

Directions

Wash and trim kale. Cut into ribbon sliced pieces.

In a large bowl mix together your black pepper, salt, olive oil, shallots, Meyer lemon zest and blood orange then put in the kale. Toss and let stand for about 20 minutes then season as desired.

Ricotta and Kale Salad

Ingredients

Ricotta
Pine Nuts
Shallots
Lemon Juice
Olive oil
Kale

Directions

Wash and trim your Kale. Tear into bite size pieces and throw into a medium size bowl. Cut up a brick of ricotta and place in the bowl with kale.

Mix together olive oil, lemon juice and shallots. Pour over your kale and massage together. Let it sit for a little bit and then top with pine nuts. Enjoy.

Kale Slaw with Peanut Dressing

Ingredients

1/2 teaspoon coarse salt
1 tablespoon packed light-brown sugar
3 tablespoons cider vinegar
1/3 cup vegetable oil
3/4 cup divided, roasted peanuts (salted)
1 large peeled carrot
2 red bell peppers clean then cut into fine strips
2 large bunches lacinato or curly kale
Pinch red pepper flakes (optional)

Directions

Finely chop your kale. Toss your kale with ½ cup peanuts, bell peppers, carrots, and red peppers.

Use a food processor to puree the rest of the peanuts with pepper and salt flakes, sugar, vinegar and oil.

Toss dressing in the bowl and let sit for a couple minutes prior to serving.

Mixed Kale Salad

Ingredients

Freshly ground black pepper to taste
1 teaspoon Dijon mustard
3 tablespoons freshly squeezed orange juice
2 tablespoons balsamic vinegar
2 tablespoons sunflower seeds
2 large mandarins (peel and cut in segments)
1/2 thinly sliced red pepper
1/2 red onion, sliced thinly
1/2 cup chopped red cabbage
1 cup chopped Tuscan kale
1 cup chopped purple kale

Directions

Mix the sunflower seeds, mandarins, red pepper, red cabbage, red onion, Tuscan kale and purple kale in a medium size bowl.

Mix together Dijon mustard, orange juice and balsamic vinegar.

Pour over the salad and toss. Season and serve.

Northern Spy Kale Salad

Ingredients

Pecorino or other hard cheese, for shaving (optional)
Fresh lemon juice
1/4 cup finely chopped or crumbled Cabot clothbound cheddar
1/4 cup almonds (cut in half)
1 bunch kale (remove ribs and slice thinly)
Freshly ground pepper and salt
Extra-virgin olive oil
1/2 cup cubed winter, butternut or kabocha squash

Directions

Trim and tear kale into a large bowl.

Cook Squash and cube, throw into bowl with the kale.

Mix all other
Ingredients
in and top with cheese.

Kale Miso Salad with Tofu

Ingredients

2 cloves minced garlic
2 tablespoons miso
2 tablespoons lemon juice
14-ounce drained package extra-firm tofu

Directions

Preheat oven to 420 and coat tofu with the above
ingredients.

Let cook for about 18-20 minutes then take out to cool.

10 Great Kale Recipes: Main Dishes

Kale and Sesame Noodles

Ingredients

1 large bunch of kale
12 oz of noodles (spaghetti, soba noodles or udon noodles can be used)
2 tablespoons sesame seeds (white or black)
Toasted sesame oil (to taste)
Tamari (to taste)

Directions

Bring a large pot of water to a boil. Cut off kale's stem. Slice kale leaves finely.

Rinse kale in large bowl to remove grit. Add pasta to large pot when water has come to a boil. Cook pasta five minutes less than directed.

Add kale to the large pot with pasta. Push leaves to

submerge in water.

Cook uncovered on high for five minutes or until both kale and pasta are tender.

Drain then add sesame oil and tamari to taste.

Toss in sesame seeds and serve.

Kale and Scallion Fried Rice

Ingredients

1 large bunch of kale
2 ½ cups of brown rice
3 large scallions
2 garlic cloves
1 ½ tablespoons of vegetable oil
1 tablespoon of soy sauce

Directions

Slice kale leaves and steam for 8 minutes. Cut scallions in 1/8 inch slices.

Peel and mince garlic cloves. Rinse rice thoroughly. Add rice into a pot with 4 ¼ cups of water. Bring to a simmer and cook for about 40 minutes. Strain rice.

On medium low heat, heat vegetable oil in a saucepan. Add garlic and cook for 2 minutes (do not brown garlic). Increase heat to medium and add kale and scallions. Cook for two minutes or so. Add rice and cook for two more minutes. Stir. Add soy sauce and stir.

Vegetarian Lasagna with Kale

Ingredients

1 lb of kale (wash, dry, remove stems and slice)
8 oz shredded mozzarella cheese (part skim)
9 lasagna noodles (oven ready)
.8 oz white sauce mix
1 tablespoon of minced garlic
Cherry or grape tomatoes (halved)
5 oz ricotta cheese
1 teaspoon olive oil
4 cups of sliced onions
Salt
Pepper

Directions

Prepare white sauce mix by following directions on packet. Heat vegetable oil in saucepan and sauté onion until golden in color. Add kale and pepper. Cook until wilted. Add a thin layer of white sauce to a baking dish.

Top with three lasagna noodles (do not overlap). Spread with ricotta cheese then layer with tomatoes, kale and sauce. Sprinkle with mozzarella cheese. Repeat once.

Top with remaining 3 lasagna noodles and cover with remaining white sauce and mozzarella cheese. Cover and bake at 375 degrees for 50 minutes.

Cajun Chicken Skillet with Kale

Ingredients

8 chicken drumsticks (skinless)
8 ounces of kielbasa sausage (cut into small bits)
1 lb of kale (remove stems and chop leaves
2 cups chicken broth
1 cup white rice (uncooked, converted)
4 teaspoons vegetable oil
1 tablespoon of cider vinegar
½ teaspoon of hot sauce
1 onion (chopped)
1 red bell pepper (cut into strips)

Directions

Heat 2 teaspoon of oil in a large nonstick skillet. Add drumsticks and cover. Turn occasionally. Cook until slightly brown. Remove from skillet and transfer to plate.

Heat remaining vegetable oil. Add bell pepper and onions. Cook until translucent. Add kale in smaller batches. When previous batch cooks down, continue to add more. Add rice and chicken broth. Stir. Place chicken on top. Add kielbasa. Stir

Cover and simmer for ten minutes. Cook until rice is tender, broth is absorbed and chicken is fully cooked. Finish off with hot sauce and cider vinegar.

Kale and Spinach Turnover

Ingredients

3 cups of kale (chopped)
1 can of refrigerated dinner roll dough
6 ounces of baby spinach (fresh)
3 ounces of crumbled feta cheese
2 ½ tablespoons grated parmesan cheese
1/8 teaspoon nutmeg (ground)
Salt
Pepper
1 clove chopped garlic
1 onion (chopped)
2 teaspoon of olive oil

Directions

Preheat the oven to 375 degrees. Heat oil in big skillet over medium flame then sauté onions or 10 minutes and put in garlic and sauté for two minutes.

Add kale and spinach and cook until tender. Add nutmeg, pepper and salt. Mix in feta cheese.

Cut dough into about 8 pieces then roll out dough into a circle 5 inches in diameter) then spoon approximately

1/3 cup of kale and spinach mixture onto the dough.

Fold over and crimp edges. Lightly coat with cooking spray and sprinkle with parmesan. Bake until golden.

Braised Chicken with Kale

Ingredients

4 skinless chicken quarters (leg)
1.1 oz flour (all purpose)
2 tablespoons canola oil
5 chopped garlic cloves
1 can fire roasted tomatoes (salt free)
16 oz kale (pre-washed)
1 can chicken broth (low sodium)
1 tablespoon vinegar (red wine)
Salt
Pepper

Directions

Preheat the oven to 350 degrees. Heat pan on medium flame then put in canola oil. Season chicken with salt and pepper then dredge in flour.

Place in pan and let cook for 2 ½ minutes on either side then remove it and add rest of oil to pan and add garlic and let cook for approximately 20 seconds.

Put in half of kale then let cook for about 2 minutes. Put in rest of kale. Cook for 3 minutes.

Add broth and tomatoes. Stir and bring to a boil. Add chicken to mixture and bake for one hour. Remove chicken. Add vinegar to kale mixture then serve.

White Bean Soup with Chorizo and Kale

Ingredients

2 oz chorizo (Spanish)
4 cups kale (chopped)
3 cup low sodium chicken broth
1 cup chopped onions
2 cans cannellini beans
3 minced garlic cloves
Black pepper

Directions

Heat large saucepan over medium flame then sauté chorizo for one minute and add onion and garlic. Cook until tender. Microwave both, for three minutes on high setting.

Add broth to pan and bring to a boil. Mash beans. Add kale and pepper to pan. Cook for 6 minutes. Serve.

Other great kale recipes include Cajun steak frites with kale, green lentil curry with kale and garbanzo beans with greens. All of these recipes are truly delicious, healthy and easy to make.

Kale with Steamed Halibut and Walnuts

Ingredients

1 1/2 pounds kale (trim stems)
2 large minced garlic cloves
1/2 cup walnuts (chopped)
3 tablespoons unsalted butter
1 thinly sliced lemon
Black pepper and kosher salt
3 tablespoons olive oil
4 6-ounce halibut fillets (skinless)

Directions

Preheat the oven to 400 degrees. Use a tablespoon oil to coat both sides of fish then place in a roasting pan.

Season with ¼ teaspoon pepper and ½ teaspoon salt then put slices of lemon on top and let roast for about fifteen minutes (fish should be opaque).

In the meantime, melt 2 tablespoons butter in a big skillet over medium flame. Put in walnuts and brown, stirring often. When done, remove from skillet and place to one side.

Put in garlic and rest of butter and oil and let cook for ½ a minute.

Put in kale, ½ teaspoon salt and ½ cup water then toss. Cover and let cook for about five minutes until kale is wilted (toss often). Mix in the walnuts and serve with the fish.

Greens and Garbanzo Beans

Ingredients

1/2 cup plain Greek yogurt (2% reduced-fat)
4 cups fresh kale (chopped)
2 cans rinsed and drained garbanzo beans (organic chickpeas)
1 cup water
2 1/2 cups fat-free chicken broth (lower-sodium)
1/2 teaspoon red pepper (crushed)
1/2 teaspoon cumin (ground)
1/4 teaspoon kosher salt
1 teaspoon paprika
2 minced garlic cloves
1/2 cup onion (chopped)
1 cup carrots (chopped)
2 slices bacon (center-cut)
4 lemon wedges (optional)

Directions

Place bacon in Dutch oven to cook until crisp then use slotted spoon to remove bacon and crumble it. Put chopped onion and 1 cup carrot in pan and let cook for about four minutes, stirring often. Put in garlic and cook for another minute, mixing often. Put in red pepper, cumin, ¼ teaspoon salt and paprika and let cook for 30 seconds while stirring often. Mix in beans, 1 cup water and chicken broth and let come to a boil then lower heat and let simmer for another twenty minutes, stirring often.

To the bean mixture add 4 cups kale then cover and let simmer until kale becomes tender (about ten minutes). In four bowls ladle approximately 1 ¼ cup bean mix then place yogurt on top (2 tablespoons). Serve with lemon wedges and sprinkle with lemon wedges if desired.

Garlic-Roasted Kale

Ingredients

1 teaspoon sherry vinegar
10 ounces chopped kale (remove stems)
1 thinly sliced garlic clove
1/4 teaspoon kosher salt
3 1/2 teaspoons olive oil (extra-virgin)

Directions

In the lower third of the oven place the oven racks then preheat the oven to 425 degrees. Put a big jelly roll pan in the oven for about five minutes.

Mix olive oil, kosher salt, sliced garlic and chopped kale in a bowl, tossing to coat. Put kale mix on the hot pan using a silicone spatula to separate the leaves. Let bake for seven minutes at 425 degrees the stir the kale. Let bake until kale is tender and edges of leaf are crispy (about five minutes).

In a big bowl place the kale, then drizzle on the vinegar and toss to mix then serve.

10 Great Kale Recipes: Desserts

When it comes to desserts health really isn't the first thing to pop into your head. Kale has been introduced into many different dessert type dishes, giving you the satisfying feeling of eating right but getting the sugar tooth satisfied. Here are a few great recipes you might enjoy.

Coconut and Chocolate Kale Chips

Ingredients

1/2 tsp cinnamon
1 tsp vanilla extract
1/3 c cocoa powder
1/2 c maple syrup/honey/agave
1/2 c soaked cashews
1 bunch of kale (remove big stems and wash)
2 tbsp coconut oil (optional)
1/4 c coconut flakes (sweetened or unsweetened) (optional)

Directions

Soak your cashews for about an hour in water. Mix the cashews and all other ingredients besides kale into a blender and mix until smooth.

Pour the mixed into a bowl over the kale until coated.

Move kale to a parchment line sheet and back in the oven at 300 degree for approximately 20 minutes. Flip them over and put back in oven for another 10 minutes.

Let cool, and enjoy

Bacon and Kale Bread Pudding

Ingredients

3/4 teaspoon pepper (freshly ground)
1 cup canned chicken broth (low sodium) or chicken stock 1 tablespoon salt
2 cups half and half or heavy cream
2 cups milk
4 large lightly beaten eggs
1 1/2 baguettes (diced- 3/4-inch thick)
2 1/2 pounds coarsely chopped kale (discard tough ribs and stems)
6 minced garlic cloves
3 finely chopped celery ribs
1 large finely chopped onion
1/2 pound sliced bacon (cut into ½ inch strips crosswise)

Directions

In a large skillet cook the bacon then put in celery and onion and keep stirring until softened. Then put in the garlic and the kale. Add into a bread bowl.

Preheat the oven to 350 degrees. Butter the dish. In a large bowl mix together eggs, milk, cream, chicken stock, and salt and pepper. Pour over the ingredients already in the bread bowl.

Bake the bread pudding for about an hour. Let stand for about 20 minutes and serve.

Kale Cake

Ingredients

1 cup walnuts
2 cups of kale
1 teaspoon vanilla
1 cup oil
1 to 1½ cups sugar
¾ cup warm water
6 tablespoons flax seed meal
½ teaspoon salt
½ teaspoon nutmeg
1 teaspoon cinnamon
1½ teaspoons baking soda
1 teaspoon baking powder
2⅓ cups all-purpose flour

Directions

Preheat oven to 350 degrees. In a large bowl mix
together all dry ingredients then add sugar and oil,
vanilla, and shocked kale and stir until moist. Add
Walnuts. Bake for about 18-20 minutes and let cool. Add
preferred icing when cake is cool.

Pesto & Kale Muffins

Ingredients

1 tablespoon lemon juice
Freshly ground black pepper
1/2 cup olive oil (extra virgin)
1/2 pound chopped raw kale (remove stems)
1/4 cup Parmigiano-Reggiano
3 large cloves garlic (trim off end and peel)
1/2 cup almonds (chopped)
2 teaspoons kosher salt

Directions

Combine all ingredients in a food processor and mix until all ingredients are chopped.

Put into muffin tins and freeze.

Kale Colada

Ingredients

Non-Dairy Frozen Dessert
1/2 Cup Coconut Milk
1 Cup Curly, Dino or Lacinato Kale
1 Cup Frozen Pineapple Chunks
1 1/2 Cup Coconut Water

Directions

Blend on a high speed until combined then serve

Kale Cookies

Ingredients

1/2 teaspoon pure vanilla extract
1/3 cup unsweetened apple sauce
2 tablespoons unsweetened plain yogurt (almond, soy, cow, goat etc)
2 tablespoons flax seed (ground) - mix with 3 tablespoons water
1 tablespoon ground ginger
1/8 teaspoon salt
1 teaspoon baking powder
1/4 cup almonds (chopped)
1/4 cup mixed pumpkin seeds, dried cranberries and raisins
1 1/2 cups kale (cook in 1 tablespoon ghee)
1 cup brown rice flour

Directions

Preheat oven to 325 degrees, Mix ingredients together, place on a baking sheet.

Bake for 20 minutes

Kale, Pancetta Pie and Butternut Squash

Ingredients

1 ounce Parmigiano-Reggiano (finely grated)
8 (17- by 12-inch) phyllo sheets (if frozen thaw)
7 tablespoons melted unsalted butter
1/4 cup water
1 1/2 pounds coarsely chopped kale (remove center ribs and stems)
2 teaspoons fresh sage (finely chopped)
3 finely chopped garlic cloves
4 slices pancetta (1/8-inch-thick)
1 medium finely chopped onion
1/2 teaspoon black pepper
3/4 teaspoon salt
1 piece butternut squash
3 tablespoons olive oil

Directions

Preheat the oven to 425 degrees
Sauté the squash with salt and pepper until brown
Then cook sage, garlic, pepper, salt, pancetta and onion stirring often. Stir in water abs kale and cover and let cook (stir occasionally).

Place mixture into shell. Spread the squash and cheese evenly over the kale mixture. Place in oven for about 20 to 25 minutes or until golden and enjoy.

Parmesan and Kale Scones

Ingredients

1 egg
3/4 cup buttermilk (whole)
1/2 cup Parmesan (grated)
1/2 cup cold butter, cut into small cubes
1 teaspoon baking soda
1/2 teaspoon salt
1 1/2 teaspoons baking powder
3 tablespoons sugar
2 1/2 cups flour (all-purpose)

Directions

Preheat oven to 425 degrees.

Combine salt, baking soda, baking powder, sugar and flour in a bowl then put in cubed butter and mix in Parmesan

In another bowl mix egg and buttermilk then start mixing in kale and keep stirring until it becomes dough, knead and flatten into 1-inch disks and cut into wedges.

Stir until the dough is properly combined. Place dough

out onto a surface that is lightly floured and knead briefly. Flatten dough into a 1-inch disk and cut into 8 wedges. Brush with butter and cook until golden.

Blueberry Kale Ice Cream

Ingredients

1/4 cup almond milk (add more if required)
5-10 pieces pineapple (frozen)
1 handful kale
1/2 cup blueberries (frozen)
1 banana (frozen)

Directions

Blend all ingredients together in a high speed blender
until thoroughly blended and serve.

Apple & Kale Muffins

Ingredients

½ cup chopped seeds or nuts
2/3 cup golden raisins
3 cups flour
1 tablespoon cinnamon
½ teaspoon salt
2 teaspoons baking soda
3/4 cup sugar
4 eggs
1 8 ounce container cream cheese (vegan)
Peel of 1 lemon
3 granny smith apples
1 small bunch kale

Directions

Preheat the oven to 350 degrees. Blend all the
ingredients until smooth then pour batter into muffin
pans then bake for 45 minutes.

About The Author

Jennifer Knight knows what it is to live a healthy life. This book focuses on one of her favorite Superfoods. This is kale.

Kale has made some resurgence in the past few years as people seek ways to eat healthy and Jennifer is more than aware of what that means.

Kale is a pretty versatile superfood and through Jennifer's book we get to learn some of the many ways that it can be used to create a fantastic meal, bit it breakfast, lunch, dinner or snack.

She pulls out all the stops as her wish is to have the reader experience kale the way she experienced it and to enjoy it just the same.

Publishers Notes

Disclaimer

This publication is intended to provide helpful and informative material. It is not intended to diagnose, treat, cure, or prevent any health problem or condition, nor is intended to replace the advice of a physician. No action should be taken solely on the contents of this book. Always consult your physician or qualified health-care professional on any matters regarding your health and before adopting any suggestions in this book or drawing inferences from it.

The author and publisher specifically disclaim all responsibility for any liability, loss or risk, personal or otherwise, which is incurred as a consequence, directly or indirectly, from the use or application of any contents of this book.

Any and all product names referenced within this book are the trademarks of their respective owners. None of these owners have sponsored, authorized, endorsed, or approved this book.

Paperback Edition 2013

Manufactured in the United States of America

Section 2: Smoothie Diet Cookbook

Smoothies are a delicious way of enjoying nature's best in fruits and vegetables. They are a great way to eat a meal in a glass, offering a fast and easy means to preparing and eating. Many people today do not get enough proper nutrition due to busy lifestyles and fast convenient foods are their mainstay. A smoothie offers a fast and convenient way to consume fresh fruits and vegetables without the added preservatives and processed sugars. Even if a person does not like the taste of vegetables, the smoothie will be covered by the flavor of the added fruit, making it easy and pleasant to consume the food.

A smoothie is a drink created from fresh fruits and vegetables with a liquid, from either water or diary or something similar. Other flavors and textures can be added if desired and it helps to make the smoothie a complete meal to add proteins.

The Benefits of a Smoothie Diet, Fruits in

Particular

The smoothies included on the smoothie diet are high in nutrients. It gives the body a good amount of vitamins and minerals and even healthful essential fatty acids when certain ingredients are included. This combination is a good way to receive the nutrients necessary to give the body energy. It takes energy to be able to move about and moving about, or exercising, is vital to a healthy body. If the desire it so lose weight, then exercising while going on the diet will help to facilitate both weight and fat loss. Smoothies offer a way to gain all the nutrients necessary in one glass, making it an easy diet to follow without a lot of prep work.

Being dehydrated is a major concern for some people. They do not take the time needed to drink the water their body needs each day. Or they drink junk food drinks that do not give the body any nutritional benefit. Being on the smoothie diet insures the body will stay well hydrated, since the smoothies are primarily liquid created from healthy foods like fruits and vegetables. Even if the main liquid of the smoothie is milk or yogurt, those are primarily made from water, so the body derives plenty of water from the drinks.

Many smoothie recipes contain dairy foods, which

makes the smoothie recipe high in calcium. Calcium is a vital nutrient and is responsible for helping the body to have strong bones. Adding milk to the recipes helps to add this nutrient to the body. When the recipe calls for yogurt, there are added benefits in the form of good probiotics, which aids the digestive system. Using whole dairy over low fat will provide a higher level of the nutrients.

The smoothie diet is one of the easiest diets to create and follow. It does not take rocket science to concoct smoothie recipes and pour them into a glass to drink. It takes significantly less time than it does to prepare food and cook a meal. Adding ingredients to the smoothies allows the offering of extra nutrients. Adding a tablespoon of extra virgin coconut oil gives a good dose of healthy fatty acids as well as antioxidants.

Breakfast is the most important meal of the day. This meal gives the energy to face the rest of the day. If we eat junk for breakfast, the result will be a sluggish feeling, and weight gain. If we eat a nutritious meal we will have energy to burn, we will want to get up and move around. Often, breakfast is overlooked due to time restraints. Busy lifestyles have us getting up late and running, unable to stop and cook a healthy breakfast. A smoothie for breakfast makes it possible to have a nutritious and quick breakfast. It only takes a few minutes to fix and drink. Much of the ingredients can be prepped the night before, so it will be ready to go the morning of. Some smoothies will allow for fixing ahead of time and storage in the refrigerator.

One of the best breakfast foods are fruit. These are packed with nutrients and have enough sweetness to them to satisfy our sweet tooth. By pairing fruit with nutritious oils and dairy, the result is a drink that will give the body energy and satisfaction. No hunger pangs, just a good feeling of wellness. Pick and choose ingredients that offer the highest level of nutrition and ones that work well together to help give the body an energy boost, which is the most important aspect of a breakfast food.

Most of the smoothie recipes do contain fruit a few contain vegetables. Fruits are high in carbohydrates. Good carbs are what gives the body the energy needed to move. Fruits contain natural sweeteners, which the body assimilates faster and easier than processed sweeteners. Caution should be made when looking to drink a prepackage smoothie over one that is home made. Prepackaged smoothies may contain added sugar and calories, which will not facilitate weight and fat loss, but will instead add to it.

The smoothie diets give the body a high amount of antioxidants, which are vital nutrients. Antioxidants are vitamins like A, C and E. These help the body to fight off free radicals. Free radicals are agents that attack the cells in the body and can lead to detrimental diseases like cancer. If the body has enough of these antioxidants, it can fight off these illnesses because it boosts and strengthens the immune system.

In addition to antioxidants, healthy smoothies also contain high levels of vital vitamins and minerals that come from the fresh foods added. All fruit is healthy, containing good levels of vitamins and minerals. Each fruit varies in the content of the nutrition; it helps to include a big variety of fruits while on the smoothie diet. For example, oranges and strawberries contain vitamin C. Cantaloupe, papaya, and peaches contain vitamin A, and B vitamins are found in bananas and cantaloupes. Bananas are known for containing potassium. Ever hear of the advice to eat a banana to keep from getting muscle spasms? Cantaloupe also contains potassium. Copper is found in kiwi, peaches, and pineapple. Bananas, blueberries, and strawberries contain manganese.

Fiber is a valuable substance in food for the body.

Without fiber the body would stop up, the digestive system would become sluggish and unable to absorb all the nutrients needed to be healthy. Fruit provides a natural source high in fiber, especially if the peels and skins of the fruit are eaten (like pears, apples and even on berries.) The meat of the fruit also contains fiber, especially kiwi, bananas and papayas and even cherries and strawberries. When eating a healthy smoothie diet be ready for a good digestive system cleanse.

A good healthy smoothie needs an added protein because fruit by itself is not too high in protein. Adding dairy, like milk or yogurt helps to provide the needed protein. Even a spoon of powdered milk will give the smoothie a nice protein boost. Protein is needed along with carbohydrates to help the body. While the carbs give energy, proteins give the cells substance, to build muscles, to move.

One of the major benefits of the smoothie diet is the low fat content in the food. Some fat is needed, so do not feel bad by choosing to use whole dairy foods. However, if you want to go lowest possible fat, choose the low fat versions of milk and yogurts.

The Benefits of Drinking Green Smoothies

Not all smoothies are made with fruit only. There is a line of smoothies that add vegetables, in particular, green veggies, thus the term "green smoothies." Going on the smoothie diet insures the body will get plenty of fruit, which is good because as discovered above, fruit contains many good nutrient. However, vegetables are just as good and contains added nutrients, some even higher in antioxidants than fruits. Many people though may turn their nose up at the thought of drinking a pureed vegetable, thinking it will not taste good. Or perhaps they feel only the diehard nutrition 'freaks' are the only ones to drink such smoothies. But the truth is vegetables are a great addition to the ingredient list for smoothie recipes. They do add their own flavors, but often, the fruit and dairy will overpower the vegetable. This allows the benefit of eating their vegetables but only tasting the fruits.

Raw vegetables are the most nutritious. When we cook vegetables, they lose some of their nutrition. Since creating smoothies requires raw ingredients, the nutrition derived from vegetables is high. The benefits of drinking a diet smoothie made with vegetables are powerful. Again, there are pre-packaged green smoothies, but often the veggies included in these are processed and pasteurized, and this causes the vegetable to lose its nutritional benefits. It is better to stick with making all smoothies from scratch to derive the most nutrition.

The diets of today, or lack of good diet, means that people are not gaining the full benefit from the foods they eat. If a person eats a lot of processed foods and junk foods, then it is likely they are not receiving any fresh fruits and vegetables. This causes a host of problems in the body starting with deficiencies of the essential vitamins and minerals we need in order to stay healthy. People think they can gain their nutrients from swallowing supplements, but the benefit is not the same. The best way for the body to get these vital nutrients are from eating highly nutritious whole foods, mainly from fruits and vegetables. Consuming green smoothies, smoothies with vegetables gives the body added vitamin A, B, C and K as well as folate, fiber, omega 3 fatty acids, iron, and zinc.

Vegetables help with weight loss and maintenance. The added vegetables in the smoothies makes them more satisfying and thus people are not as hunger after consuming them and are able to make it to their next snack or meal without being too hungry in between. A really good green smoothie will have sixty-percent fruit with forty percent vegetables. This combination makes the food easier to digest and the body gains the benefit of the nutrients as a result. Junk foods go through the body faster and thus hunger comes on faster, but also because of junk food, the body is not able to absorb all the nutrients from the foods. Eating fruits and vegetables, especially in raw form, slows down the digestive process just enough that the body is able to absorb all the proper nutrients. It also gives a fuller feeling longer, curbing the hunger and stopping the need to graze and snack. In essence, the more junk food you eat, the hungrier you will be and you will keep eating more to try to satisfy the hunger.

Smoothies are actually very good to taste. This is why so many enjoy making smoothies for quickie breakfasts and snacks regardless of their main diet. So many people do not like the taste of vegetables and smoothies, especially green smoothies, give the opportunity to include vegetables without the worry of the taste hindering the enjoyment of it. Because smoothies are more fruit, the fruit flavor overpowers the vegetable flavor.

Lose Weight and Fat on the Smoothie Diet

The smoothie diet makes it easy to lose weight and body fat because of the ease in both the creation of smoothies and the ease of drinking them. It is almost too easy, but once a person starts the smoothie diet and sees how easy it is they may have to force themselves to eat whole foods again.

If you eat smoothies for each meal, you will want to try to incorporate more protein by adding protein powder (found at health food stores). A spoon or two of this and it makes the smoothie a complete meal. Feel free to add extra foods to the recipes, if you want the recipe sweeter, try throwing in some extra ripe pieces of fruits, especially berries, will add to the sweetness factor.

Smoothie Creations - A Quick How To Guide

The star of the smoothie creation is the blender. You cannot make a decent smoothie without one, so if you do not have one, go purchase one. You can use a food processor too if that is all you have. You will want a decent blender, one that will be able to handle pureeing whole pieces of fruit and vegetables.

Fresh fruit and vegetables are always the best, however, frozen will work just as well. Sometimes fresh fruits and vegetables may not be available, so you will have to turn to frozen. Canned fruits and vegetables can work in a pinch, but only if you absolutely cannot find them in fresh or frozen form. Remember canned foods are processed and cooked and have lost some of their nutrients in the process.

Some fruits and maybe a few vegetables may contain enough juice to create a good smoothie, providing all the liquid needed. However, some do not and the addition of a liquid is needed. Many smoothie recipes call for milk or yogurt. Some may use water and some may use a dairy substitute. This gives some protein in the mix as well. Other "liquid" choices include nut milks, tea, actual fruit juice, ice cream, yogurt, sparkling water, and plain water.

If you are on a smoothie diet and drinking them with every meal or in place of every meal, you will want to sprinkle protein powder in the mix. Protein powder is made from soy, rice, and whey.

A well-balanced smoothie meal will have fruit, vegetables, and protein. Even if you are making one of the fruit only recipes, you can add some sneaky vegetables into the mix and no one will be the wiser. Sneak in a bit of chopped spinach or kale. Try some celery or even beetroot. If you cannot find fresh vegetables, visit your local health food store and purchase green plant powder, and add a spoonful of this to turn the fruit smoothie into a green smoothie.

If you want the smoothie to taste sweeter instead of grabbing for the sugar bowl try some of these suggestions: a ripe banana, a spoonful or two of honey, stevia, or agave nectar.

Do you want to spice up the smoothie or give it more flavor? Try adding some extra ingredients that add a burst of flavor like vanilla extract, cayenne pepper, almond extract, coconut milk, cinnamon, salt, or a spoonful of nut butter.

If you enjoy a thicker and colder smoothie try crushing ice and including it in the blender. Only do this when you plan to drink the smoothie right then. You cannot store smoothies with ice chunks for too long in the refrigerator or the smoothie will be too thin and runny. Some smoothies may be good as frozen pops, experiment with this, especially if it is hot weather, and if you enjoy frozen pops.

If your blender is new, you may need to experiment with the settings to figure out which ones will work best for the smoothie recipes. Sometimes you may need to puree to get the desired texture, while other times just the blend setting will work.

Just because you are on the smoothie diet does not mean you cannot enjoy whole foods too. If you have made a smoothie using berries, save a few for garnishment once the smoothie is done. You can also garnish with a different fruit or even a wedge of lemon or a mint sprig or parsley leaf (depending on whether or not the smoothie is sweet or savory.)

Tips for Making Good Smoothies

If you find you have a fruit or vegetable that is difficult to blend into a drink, try "juicing" it first. You will need a juicer in order to do this. Juicers are able to handle turning even the toughest pieces of fruit and vegetables into a liquid. If you do not own a juicer, try peeling the fruit or vegetable first. Blend the center first. Chop the peel into fine pieces and add it a little bit at a time until the smoothie is at the consistency you desire. Always chop the fruit and vegetables before adding to the blender.

If the smoothie is too thin, try adding a bit more fruit, or ice cubes. If it is too thick, thin it with liquid, milk, yogurt, ice cream, or even fruit juice or water. If you wish for a creamy smoothie use yogurt or ice cream for the liquid instead of water and ice.

It is okay to refrigerate or even freeze a smoothie if you cannot consume it right after creating it. Allow a frozen smoothie to thaw in the refrigerator for a day, or allow it to sit out at room temperature for about an hour. If you refrigerate it, drink it within a day.

If you plan to use fruit juice for the liquid try freezing it in ice trays first, that way it will help the smoothie to have a thicker frozen texture.

When blending the smoothie always test a spoonful first to make sure of the flavor and texture before pouring into a glass.

Note: Most of the recipes within this book are for 1 serving, since these types of diets are normally enjoyed by one person at a time. It is easy to double or triple or more each recipe as needed. Always peel bananas and discard the peel. Always cut the leaves from the fruit, such as the tops of strawberries.

Measurement Help: 1 banana equals 1/3 cup.

Fruit Smoothies

Peanut Banana Berry Smoothie

A nutritious smoothie that provides omega 3 fatty acids from flax seed meal.

Makes 1 serving.

Ingredients:

*1/2 cup of milk
*1/4 cup of banana (ripe)
*1/4 cup of blueberries (fresh or frozen)
*1/4 cup of yogurt (plain)
*1/2 tablespoon of flax seed meal
*1/2 tablespoon of peanut butter
*1/2 teaspoon of honey

Directions:

First, grind the 1/2 tablespoon of flax seed meal into a fine powder. Next, add the 1/2 cup of milk, 1/4 cup of ripe banana, 1/4 cup of blueberries, 1/4 cup of plain yogurt, 1/2 tablespoon of peanut butter and the 1/2 teaspoon of honey into a blender and blend until the texture you desire. Pour into a glass and enjoy.

Blackberry Banana Smoothie

It is hard to beat the sweet flavor of fresh ripe blackberries (or frozen if they are not in season).

Makes 1 serving.

Ingredients:

*1/2 cup of ice (crushed)
*1/4 cup of blackberries (fresh is best, but frozen will work) + 3 whole blackberries
*1/4 cup of banana (ripe)
*1/8 cup of orange juice
*2 strawberries
*1/4 teaspoon of honey

Directions:

Add the 1/2 cup of crushed ice, 1/4 cup of blackberries, 1/4 cup of ripe banana, 1/4 cup of orange juice, and the 1/4 teaspoon of honey. Cut the top off the strawberries and cut them in half, add to the blender. Blend until smooth. Pour into a glass and garnish with the 3 blackberries.

Spicy Banana Smoothie

Here is a banana smoothie with some spice from cinnamon and a bit of nuttiness from almond butter.

Makes 1 serving.

Ingredients:

*1 banana
*1 1/2 cups of almond milk
*1/4 cup of almond butter
*2 tablespoons of honey
*1 tablespoon of cinnamon (ground)

Directions:

PREP: First, freeze the banana, and then once frozen, peel and chop it into bits.

Once the banana is prepared, pour the 1 1/2 cups of almond milk into the blender and add the 1/4 cup of almond butter, 2 tablespoons of honey, and the tablespoon of ground cinnamon. Blend until smooth, then add the chopped frozen banana and blend until the texture you desire. Pour into a glass and enjoy.

Watermelon Banana Berry Smoothie

There is nothing quite as refreshing as this smoothie, it is best made in the summer when the watermelons are plentiful and sweet.

Makes 1 serving.

Ingredients:

*1/2 cup of cranberry juice
*1/2 cup of strawberries
*1/4 cup of blueberries
*1/4 cup of watermelon (chunked)
*1/4 cup of banana (ripe)
*1/2 of a fig

Directions:

Add the 1/2 cup of cranberry juice to a blender along with the 1/2 cup of strawberries, 1/4 cup of blueberries, 1/4 cup of chunked watermelon, 1/4 cup of ripe banana and the 1/2 fig. Blend until it reaches desired texture. Pour into a glass and enjoy.

Mango Papaya Smoothie

Mango paired with papaya and mixed with orange and lime makes for a delicious tropical smoothie.

Makes 1 serving.

Ingredients:

*1/2 cup of water
*1/8 cup of papaya (peeled and diced)
*1/8 cup of mango (sliced)
*1/8 cup of orange juice
*1/2 tablespoon of lime juice
*1/2 tablespoon of honey
*1/8 teaspoon of orange zest
*glass of crushed ice

Directions:

First step, add the 1/8 cup of peeled, diced papaya and the 1/8 cup of sliced mango into the blender. Puree. Add the 1/8 cup of orange juice, 1/2 tablespoon of lime juice, 1/2 tablespoon of honey and 1/8 teaspoon of orange zest and blend until smooth. Pour over the crushed ice and enjoy.

Banana Coconut Smoothie

This tropical smoothie is extra sweet with ice cream.

Makes 1 serving.

Ingredients:

*1 1/2 scoop of vanilla ice cream
*1 banana (ripe)
*1/2 cup of coconut milk
*1 teaspoon of honey

Directions:

Add the 1 1/2 scoops of vanilla ice cream along with the ripe banana, 1/2 cup of coconut milk and teaspoon of honey to a blender. Blend until smooth. Pour into glass and enjoy.

Fruit Spread Smoothie

This smoothie uses 2 tablespoons of your favorite all natural fruit spread. Fruit spread is not just for bread! Makes 1 serving.

Ingredients:

*1/2 cup of milk
*1/4 cup of yogurt (plain)
*1/4 cup of strawberries (fresh or frozen, sliced)
*2 tablespoons of all-natural fruit spread (your favorite flavor)
*1 tablespoon of oats

Directions:

Add the 1/2 cup of milk, 1/4 cup of plain yogurt, 1/4 cup of sliced strawberries, 2 tablespoons of your favorite all-natural fruit spread and 1 tablespoon of oats to the blender. Blend until it reaches desired consistency. Pour in a glass and enjoy.

Nothing But Fruit Smoothie

The thing that sets this smoothie a part from others is the presence of nothing but fruit in the mix.

Makes 1 serving.

Ingredients:

*1/3 cup of banana (chunked)
*1/2 cup of strawberries (frozen)
*1/2 cup of blueberries (frozen)
*1/2 cup of pineapple juice

Directions:

First, pour the 1/2 cup of pineapple juice in the blender and add the 1/3 cup of chunked bananas. Blend until smooth. Add the 1/2 cup of frozen strawberries and the 1/2 cup of frozen blueberries and blend until desired texture is achieved. Pour into glass and enjoy.

Creamy Strawberry Smoothie

Strawberries are the star of this delicious creamy smoothie.

Makes 1 serving.

Ingredients:

*1/4 cup of milk
*1/4 cup of yogurt (plain)
*4 strawberries
*3 ice cubes (crushed)
*1 1/2 tablespoons of honey
*1 teaspoon of vanilla extract

Directions:

Add the 1/4 cup of milk, 1/4 cup of plain yogurt, 4 strawberries, 3 crushed ice cubes, 1 1/2 tablespoons of honey, and teaspoon of vanilla extract into a blender and blend until smooth. Pour into a glass and enjoy.

Apple Spice Smoothie

This smoothie is made from applesauce, making it extra creamy.

Makes 1 serving.

Ingredients:

*1 cup of applesauce
*1/2 cup of apple cider
*1/2 cup of orange juice
*1 tablespoon of maple syrup
*1/4 teaspoon of nutmeg (ground)
*1/4 teaspoon of cinnamon (ground)

Directions:

Add the 1 cup of applesauce in a blender along with the 1/2 cup of apple cider, 1/2 cup of orange juice, tablespoon of maple syrup, 1/4 teaspoon of ground nutmeg, and the 1/4 teaspoon of ground cinnamon. Blend until smooth and serve in a glass.

Banana Berry Vanilla Smoothie

A delicious and creamy banana and blueberry smoothies.

Makes 1 serving.

Ingredients:

*1 cup of soy milk (vanilla)
*3/4 cup of bananas (sliced)
*1/2 cup of blueberries (frozen)
*1/2 cup of yogurt (vanilla)

Directions:

Prep: Slice the banana (after peeling) and freeze the slices.

In a blender, add the 1 cup of vanilla soy milk, 3/4 cup of frozen sliced bananas, 1/2 cup of frozen blueberries, and the 1/2 cup of vanilla yogurt. Blend well and pour into a glass and serve.

Refreshing Smoothie

This smoothie is refreshing with a taste of lemon in the mix.

Makes 1 serving.

Ingredients:

*1 cup of yogurt (vanilla)
*1/4 cup of banana (chunked)
*3 strawberries (cut up and frozen)
*1/2 tablespoon of honey
*1/4 teaspoon of vanilla extract
*1/4 teaspoon of lemon juice
*ice

Directions:

Add the cup of vanilla yogurt, 1/4 cup of chunked banana, 3 cut up and frozen strawberries, 1/2 tablespoon of honey, 1/4 teaspoon of vanilla extract, and 1/4 teaspoon of lemon juice in a blender and blend well. Add enough ice and blend more to get the smoothie to the texture you desire. Pour in a glass and enjoy.

Peachy Banana Berry Vanilla Smoothie

The flavors dance on the palate, bananas, orange, vanilla, peach and strawberry.

Makes 1 serving.

Ingredients:

*3/4 cup of yogurt (vanilla)
*1/2 cup of strawberries (frozen)
*1/3 cup of peaches (frozen)
*1/4 cup of banana
*1/2 tablespoon of orange juice (from frozen concentrate can)
In a blender add the 3-4 cup of vanilla yogurt, 1/2 cup of frozen strawberries, 1/3 cup of frozen peaches, 1/4 cup of bananas and the 1/2 tablespoon of frozen orange juice concentrate and blend until smooth. Pour in a glass and enjoy.

Extra Large Fruit Punch Smoothie

This is a delightful smoothie created with all the fun fruits of summer.

Makes one extra-large serving, or 2 small servings.

Ingredients:

*1/2 cup of ice
*1/2 cup of ice cream (vanilla)
*1/3 cup of strawberries (frozen)
*1/3 cup of all natural fruit punch
*1/4 cup of banana
*1/4 cup of peach nectar
*1 strawberry sliced (garnishment)

In a blender, add the 1/2 cup of ice, 1/2 cup of vanilla ice cream, 1/3 cup of frozen strawberries, 1/3 cup of all natural fruit punch, 1/4 cup of bananas, 1/4 cup of peach nectar and blend until smooth consistency. Pour into a tall glass and garnish with strawberry slices if desired.

Raspberry Banana Smoothie

Enjoy this smoothie lightly flavored with frozen raspberries and bananas.

Makes 1 serving.

*3/4 cup of almond milk (sweetened)
*1/2 cup of frozen raspberries
*1/2 cup of yogurt (vanilla)
*1/4 cup of banana (chunked and frozen)

In a blender, add the 3/4 cup of sweetened almond milk, 1/2 cup of frozen raspberries, 1/2 cup of vanilla yogurt, and the 1/4 cup of chunked frozen bananas and blend until smooth. Pour in glass and enjoy.

Mango Banana Smoothie

A unique and delicious combination with the mango and banana.

Makes 1 serving.

Ingredients:

*1/2 cup of yogurt (vanilla)
*1/2 cup of orange juice (fresh squeezed)
*1/4 cup of banana
*1 mango

Peel and remove the pit in the mango. Chop it, put into a blender along with the 1/2 cup of vanilla yogurt, 1/2 cup of fresh squeezed orange juice, and the 1/4 cup of banana, and blend until smooth. Pour into a glass and enjoy.

Vanilla Orange Banana Smoothie

A delicious cream sickle flavored smoothie.

Makes 1 extra-large serving.

Ingredients:

*1/2 cup of yogurt (vanilla)
*1/2 cup of orange juice (fresh squeezed)
*1/2 cup of ice
*1/4 cup of milk
*1/4 cup of banana
*2 tablespoons of honey

Add the 1/2 cup of vanilla yogurt, 1/2 cup of fresh squeezed orange juice, 1/2 cup of ice, 1/4 cup of milk, 1/4 cup of bananas along with the 2 tablespoons of honey in a blender and blend until smooth. Pour in a glass and enjoy.

Purple Smoothie

Purple in color from the mix of red strawberries, orange and blue from blueberries.

Makes 1 serving.

Ingredients:

*1/2 cup of yogurt (plain)
*1/4 cup of strawberries
*1/8 cup of blueberries (frozen)
*1/8 cup of bananas (chunked)
*1/8 cup of orange juice
*1/4 tablespoon of soy milk powder

Directions:

Add the 1/2 cup of plain yogurt, 1/4 cup of strawberries, 1/8 cup of frozen blueberries, 1/8 cup of chunked bananas, 1/8 cup of orange juice and the 1/4 tablespoon of soy milk powder to a blender and blend until smooth. Pour in a glass and enjoy.

Fruit Milky Smoothie

A very simple smoothie with four simple ingredients, this is a can't go wrong recipe.

Makes 1 serving.

*1/2 cup of apples (chopped, peeled and cored)
*1/4 cup of orange juice
*1/8 cup of bananas (frozen chopped)
*1/8 cup of milk

Directions:

Chop the apple into fine chunks and add 1/2 cup to a blender along with 1/4 cup of orange juice, 1/8 cup of frozen chopped bananas, and 1/8 cup of milk. Blend until smooth and pour into a glass to serve.

Strawberry Pear Smoothie

A perfect smoothie to enjoy when the fruit harvest comes through in the summer.

Makes 1 serving.

Ingredients:

*1/2 of a pair (cubed and cored)
*1/3 cup of yogurt (vanilla)
*1/4 cup of ice
*1/8 cup of milk
*1 strawberry
*1 teaspoon of honey

Directions:

Add the 1/4 cup of ice in the bottom of the blender then add the 1/2 of a cubed pear, along with the 1/3 cup of vanilla yogurt, 1/8 cup of milk, hulled strawberry and the teaspoon of honey. Blend until smooth, pour into a glass, and enjoy.

Spicy Banana Smoothie

Combine the flavors of banana with orange, raspberry and nutmeg and enjoy the flavor explosion in your mouth.

Makes 1 serving.

Ingredients:

*1/4 cup of yogurt (raspberry)
*1/4 cup of bananas (chunked and frozen)
*1/4 cup of an orange (chopped and peeled)
*1/2 tablespoon of honey
*1/8 teaspoon of nutmeg (ground)

Directions:

In a blender, add the 1/4 cup of raspberry yogurt with the 1/4 cup of chunked frozen bananas, 1/4 cup of chopped, peeled orange, 1/2 tablespoon of honey and 1/8 teaspoon of ground nutmeg and blend until smooth. Pour into a glass and enjoy.

PB Banana Smoothie

This is a delightful smoothie that combines the wonderful flavor of peanut butter with banana to bring the timeless classic combination to a smoothie.

Makes 1 serving.

Ingredients:

*1/4 cup of milk
*1/4 cup of banana (chunked)
*1/8 cup of peanut butter (creamy)
*1 tablespoon of honey
*3 ice cubes

Directions:

Add the 1/4 cup of milk into a blender along with 1/4 cup of chunked banana, 1/8 cup of creamy peanut butter, tablespoon of honey and 3 ice cubes and blend until smooth. Pour in glass and serve immediately.

Herbed Strawberry Mango Smoothie

This fruity smoothie comes complete with a basil kick.

Makes 1 serving.

Ingredients:

*5 strawberries (chopped)
*4 basil leaves (fresh)
*3 ice cubes
*1 cup of cold water
*1 cup of mango (frozen, chunked)
*2 tablespoons of honey

Directions:

Add the 5 chopped strawberries, 4 fresh basil leaves, cup of cold water, cup of frozen chunked mango to the blender and blend. Add the 3 ice cubes and 2 tablespoons of honey and blend for a few more seconds to disperse the ice. Pour into a glass and enjoy.

Orange Berry All Fruit Smoothie

This refreshing smoothie makes a great snack or dessert.

Makes 1 serving.

Ingredients:

*3/4 cup of strawberries (frozen)
*1/4 cup of orange juice
*1 tablespoon of raspberries (frozen)

Directions:

Blend the 3/4 cup of frozen strawberries, 1/4 cup of orange juice, and the 1 tablespoon of frozen raspberries until smooth. Pour into a glass and enjoy.

Berry Berry Smoothie

Berries are everywhere in this delicious, all berry smoothie, which makes for a great snack.

Makes 1 serving.

Ingredients:

*1 cup of berries (you choose, mix them up- raspberries, strawberries, blackberries)
*5 ice cubes
*1/8 cup of water
*1/8 cup of all berry all natural fruit juice
*1/8 cup of raspberries (frozen)
*1/8 cup of blueberries (frozen)

Directions:

Add the 5 ice cubes to the blender and crush before adding the 1/8 cup of cold water and the 1/8 cup of berry juice. Blend a few seconds then add the cup of mixed berries along with the 1/8 cup of frozen raspberries and the 1/8 cup of frozen blueberries, blend until smooth, and serve immediately.

Blueberry Banana Protein Smoothie

This is a good meal replacement smoothie because of the added protein powder, blueberry and banana flavor.

Makes 1 serving.

Ingredients:

*1/2 cup of soymilk (vanilla)
*1/2 cup of blueberries (frozen)
*1/4 cup of bananas (chunked and frozen)
*1/4 cup of ice cubes
*1/2 tablespoon of soy protein powder
*1/2 teaspoon of honey

Directions:

Add the 1/2 cup of soymilk (vanilla), 1/2 cup of blueberries (frozen), 1/4 cup of bananas (chunked and frozen), 1/4 cup of ice cubes, 1/2 tablespoon of soy protein powder, and the 1/2 teaspoon of honey to a blender and blend until smooth. Pour in a glass and enjoy.

Mango Blueberry Smoothie

A delicious smoothie strong on mango and blueberry flavor with a hint of vanilla.

Makes 1 serving.

Ingredients:

*1/2 cup of yogurt (vanilla)
*1/2 cup of mango juice
*1/4 cup of blueberries (frozen)
*1/4 cup of mango (frozen chunks)
*1 tablespoon of chia seeds (fine ground)
*1/2 teaspoon of vanilla extract

Directions:

Add the 1/2 cup of yogurt (vanilla), 1/2 cup of mango juice, 1/4 cup of blueberries (frozen), 1/4 cup of mango (frozen chunks), 1 tablespoon of chia seeds (fine ground), and the 1/2 teaspoon of vanilla extract into a blender and blend until smooth. Pour into a glass and enjoy.

Tapioca Chai Smoothie

This smoothie needs a spoon to enjoy the tapioca pearls.

Makes 1 serving.

Ingredients:

*1 cup of ice
*1/2 cup of tapioca pearls
*1/2 cup of milk
*1/2 cup of chai tea (mix)
*1 1/2 tablespoon of honey (divided)

Directions:

Prep: In a small saucepan, add water to fill half the pan. Turn heat to high and bring water to a boil. Add the 1/2 cup of tapioca pearls and bring the water to a second boil, stirring continually. Place a lid on the saucepan, turn the heat to medium, and set timer for 45 minutes. Take the saucepan off the stove, but keep the lid on, allow to sit for an extra half an hour to cool. Pour the pearls out into a strainer and rinse under cool water. Place the tapioca in a bowl, drizzle the 1 tablespoon of honey over, and toss.

Pour the 1 cup of ice and 1/2 cup of milk into a blender along with the 1/2 cup of chai tea mix and 1/2 tablespoon of honey and blend until slushy. Pour the smoothie into a glass, then add the honey coated tapioca pearls and stir. Enjoy.

Refreshingly Fruity Smoothie

Enjoy the flavors of almond with cherry, banana and oranges in this smoothie.

Makes 1 serving.

Ingredients:

*1/2 cup of yogurt (cherry)
*1/2 cup of mandarin oranges
*1/4 cup of banana (chunked)
*1/8 cup of half-and-half cream
*1/2 teaspoon of almond extract
*1 cherry

Directions:

Add in a blender the 1/2 cup of yogurt (cherry), 1/2 cup of mandarin oranges, 1/4 cup of banana (chunked), 1/8 cup of half-and-half cream, and the 1/2 teaspoon of almond extract and blend until smooth. Pour into a glass and garnish with the cherry. Enjoy.

Cherry Lemon Banana Smoothie

What do you get when you combine lemon with cherries and bananas? This delicious smoothie.

Makes 1 serving.

Ingredients:

*1/2 cup of cherries (frozen and pitted)
*1/4 cup of banana (chunked)
*1/4 cup of Greek yogurt
*3 ice cubes
*lemon juice (from a piece of a quartered lemon)
*1/8 teaspoon of almond extract

Directions:

In a blender add the 1/2 cup of cherries (frozen and pitted), 1/4 cup of banana (chunked), 1/4 cup of Greek yogurt, 3 ice cubes, lemon juice (from a piece of a quartered lemon), and 1/8 teaspoon of almond extract and blend until smooth. Pour into a glass and enjoy.

Berry Good Cherry Smoothie

Cherries, raspberries and red grapes make this an extra sweet delicious smoothie.

Makes 1 serving.

Ingredients:

*1/3 cup of cherry juice
*1/3 cup of yogurt (vanilla)
*1/3 cup of raspberries (frozen)
*1/8 cup of grapes (red, seedless)
*1 teaspoon of honey

Directions:

Add in a blender 1/3 cup of cherry juice, 1/3 cup of yogurt (vanilla), 1/3 cup of raspberries (frozen), 1/8 cup of grapes (red, seedless), and 1 teaspoon of honey and blend until smooth. Pour in a glass and enjoy.

Hot Chocolate Strawberry Smoothie

Don't let the name fool you, this smoothie is plenty cool and strawberry, but starts with a nice shot of hot chocolate.

Makes 1 serving.

Ingredients:

*1 cup of milk
*4 tablespoons of strawberries (frozen)
*4 ice cubes
*2 teaspoons of cocoa powder
*1 teaspoon of honey
*1 teaspoon of hot water

Directions:

First, in a cup, mix the teaspoon of hot water with the 2 teaspoons of cocoa powder to make a smooth paste. Next, add the 1 cup of milk, 4 tablespoons of strawberries (frozen), 4 ice cubes, and the 1 teaspoon of honey in a blender and stir in the cocoa paste. Blend until smooth, pour in a glass and enjoy.

Hot Chocolate Blueberry Smoothie

Don't let the name fool you, this smoothie is plenty cool and blueberry, but starts with a nice shot of hot chocolate.

Makes 1 serving.

Ingredients:

*1 cup of milk
*4 tablespoons of blueberries (frozen)
*4 ice cubes
*2 teaspoons of cocoa powder
*1 teaspoon of honey
*1 teaspoon of hot water

Directions:

First, in a cup, *mix* the teaspoon of hot water with the 2 teaspoons of cocoa powder to make a smooth paste. Next, add the 1 cup of milk, 4 tablespoons of blueberries (frozen), 4 ice cubes, and the 1 teaspoon of honey in a blender and stir in the cocoa paste. Blend until smooth, pour in a glass and enjoy.

Banana Cherry Cordial Smoothie

This is certainly a delightful dessert or snack smoothie.

Makes 1 serving.

Ingredients:

*1/2 cup of cherries (pitted and frozen)
*1/2 cup of chocolate milk
*1/4 cup of bananas (frozen chunks)

Directions:

In a blender, add 1/2 cup of cherries (pitted and frozen), 1/2 cup of chocolate milk, and 1/4 cup of bananas (frozen chunks) and blend until smooth. Pour in a glass and enjoy.

Simple Chocolate Peanut Butter Banana Smoothie

All the flavors loved by so many wrapped into a delicious smoothie.

Makes 1 serving.

Ingredients:

*1/2 cup of milk
*1/4 cup of banana (chunked)
*2 tablespoons of peanut butter (creamy)
*2 tablespoons of chocolate syrup

Directions:

In a blender, add 1/2 cup of milk, 1/4 cup of banana (chunked), 2 tablespoons of peanut butter (creamy), and 2 tablespoons of chocolate syrup and blend until smooth. Pour in a glass and enjoy.

Acai Cinnamon Berry Smoothie

This smoothie packs a little more punch with the inclusion of egg whites in the mix.

Makes 1 serving.

Ingredients:

*1/2 cup of acai juice
*1/4 cup of strawberries (frozen)
*1/8 cup of pasteurized liquid egg whites
*1/8 cup of apple cider
*1 tablespoon of honey
*1/3 tablespoon of cocoa powder
*1/4 tablespoon of cinnamon (ground)
*1/4 teaspoon of turmeric

Directions:

In a blender add 1/2 cup of acai juice, 1/4 cup of strawberries (frozen), 1/8 cup of pasteurized liquid egg whites, 1/8 cup of apple cider, 1 tablespoon of honey, 1/3 tablespoon of cocoa powder, 1/4 tablespoon of cinnamon (ground), and 1/4 teaspoon of turmeric and blend until smooth. Pour in a glass and enjoy.

Spicy Pear Smoothie

A delightful variation with your favorite smoothie drinks with pears.

Makes 1 serving.

Ingredients:

*1 pear (cored and chunked)
*1/2 cup of milk
*1/4 cup of banana (chunked)
*1/4 cup of yogurt (vanilla)
*1 teaspoon of cinnamon (ground)
*shake of nutmeg (ground)

Directions:

In a blender, add 1 pear (cored and chunked), 1/2 cup of milk, 1/4 cup of banana (chunked), 1/4 cup of yogurt (vanilla), 1 teaspoon of cinnamon (ground), and shake of nutmeg (ground) and blend until smooth. Pour in a glass and enjoy.

Sweet Banana Nut Smoothie

Couple banana with coconut and you get this delicious and sweet smoothie.

Makes 1 serving.

Ingredients:

*1/2 cup of coconut milk
*1/2 cup of bananas (chunked)
*1 1/2 scoops of ice cream (vanilla)
*1 teaspoon of honey

Directions:

In a blender, add 1/2 cup of coconut milk, 1/2 cup of bananas (chunked), 1 1/2 scoops of ice cream (vanilla), and 1 teaspoon of honey and blend until smooth. Pour in a glass and enjoy.

Hot Chocolate Dessert Smoothie

This smoothie is too decadent to be called anything but a dessert.

Makes 1 serving.

Ingredients:

*1 1/2 cups of milk
*1 1/2 scoops of ice cream (vanilla)
*1/4 cup of whipped cream
*2 tablespoons of hot cocoa mix
*5 cookies (your favorite kind that goes well with chocolate - crushed)
*extra whipped topping
*extra crushed cookies

Directions:

In a blender add 1 1/2 cups of milk, 1 1/2 scoops of ice cream (vanilla), 1/4 cup of whipped cream, 2 tablespoons of hot cocoa mix , 5 cookies (crushed) and blend until smooth. Pour in a glass and enjoy. Garnish with whipped topping and a sprinkling of crushed cookies.

Orange Berry Banana Smoothie

This is a delicious combination of orange, cranberry, banana, strawberry and raspberry flavors.

Makes 1 servings.

Ingredients:

*1/2 cup of cranberry juice
*1/2 cup of ice cubes
*1/4 cup of banana (chunked)
*1/4 cup of strawberries (sliced and hulled)
*1/8 cup of sherbet (raspberry)
*1/8 cup of whey protein powder
*1/2 of an orange (peeled and quartered)

Directions:

In a blender add 1/2 cup of cranberry juice, 1/2 cup of ice cubes, 1/4 cup of banana (chunked), 1/4 cup of strawberries (sliced and hulled), 1/8 cup of sherbet (raspberry), 1/8 cup of whey protein powder, and 1/2 of an orange (peeled and quartered) and blend until smooth. Pour in a glass and enjoy.

Fig Smoothie

A different flavor for smoothies, this one will be a favorite.

Makes 1 serving.

*10 figs
*1/2 cup of yogurt (vanilla Greek)
*1/2 cup of coconut milk
*1/2 cup of ice cubes
*1/4 cup of water
*1 tablespoon of flaxseed oil
*1 teaspoon of cinnamon (ground)

Directions:

In a blender add 10 figs, 1/2 cup of yogurt (vanilla Greek), 1/2 cup of coconut milk, 1/2 cup of ice cubes, 1/4 cup of water, 1 tablespoon of flaxseed oil, and 1 teaspoon of cinnamon (ground) and blend until smooth. Pour in a glass and enjoy.

Minty Melon-Umber Smoothie

This refreshing smoothie combines the delicious tastes of honeydew melon with a refreshing cucumber and fresh mint.

Makes 1 serving.

Ingredients:

*1/2 of a cumber (peeled, seeds removed and sliced)
*4 mint sprigs
*1 cup of ice (crushed)
*1 cup of honeydew melon (cubed)
*1 cup of passion fruit juice

Directions:

Prep: Remove the stems from the mint sprigs. Then in a blender add 1/2 of a cumber (peeled, seeds removed and sliced), 4 mint sprigs, 1 cup of ice (crushed), 1 cup of honeydew melon (cubed), and 1 cup of passion fruit juice and blend until smooth. Pour into a glass and enjoy.

Tangerine Smoothie

Not only will you enjoy the flavor of refreshing tangerine but also dragon fruit and lime with a touch of basil.

Makes 1 serving.

Ingredients:

*1 tangerine (peeled and quartered)
*2 basil leaves
*1/2 of a dragon fruit
*1/2 of a lime (juice only)
*1/2 cup of sparkling mineral water (cold)
*1/2 cup of ice (crushed)
*1 tablespoon of honey

Directions:

In a blender add 1 tangerine (peeled and quartered), 2 basil leaves, 1/2 of a dragon fruit, 1/2 of a lime (juice only), 1/2 cup of sparkling mineral water (cold), 1/2 cup of ice (crushed), and 1 tablespoon of honey and blend until smooth. Pour into a glass and enjoy.

Sweet Mango Smoothie

This is a delicious mango smoothie to satisfy the sweet tooth.

Makes 1 serving.

Ingredients:

*1/2 cup of yogurt
*1/4 cup of milk
*3/4 of a mango (peeled, seeds removed and chunked)
*1 teaspoon of honey
*dash of cardamom (ground)

Directions:

In a blender add 1/2 cup of yogurt, 1/4 cup of milk, 3/4 of a mango (peeled, seeds removed and chunked), and 1 teaspoon of honey and blend until smooth. Pour into a glass and place in the refrigerator for an hour. Sprinkle a dash of ground cardamom and serve.

Almond Banana Smoothie

When you combine almond butter with bananas, you get a delicious smoothie complete with a hint of cinnamon.

Makes 1 serving.

*1 banana (chunked and frozen)
*1 cup of milk
*1/2 tablespoon of almond butter
*1/2 teaspoon of vanilla extract
*dash of ground cinnamon

Directions:

In a blender, add 1 banana (chunked), 1 cup of milk, 1/2 tablespoon of almond butter, and 1/2 teaspoon of vanilla extract and blend until smooth. Pour into a glass and garnish with a dash of ground cinnamon. Enjoy.

Pumpkin Smoothie

Here is a delicious autumn smoothie that can be enjoyed year round because it calls for canned pumpkin puree.

Makes 1 serving.

Ingredients:

*1/2 cup of milk
*1/4 cup of pumpkin puree (frozen)
*1 tablespoon of honey
*1/2 teaspoon of cinnamon (ground)

Directions:

In a blender, add 1/2 cup of milk, 1/4 cup of frozen pumpkin puree, 1 tablespoon of honey, and 1/2 teaspoon of cinnamon (ground) and blend until smooth. Pour in a glass and enjoy.

Oatmeal and Fruit Smoothie

This is a stick to your ribs, satisfying smoothie.

Makes 1 serving.

Ingredients:

*1/2 cup of milk
*1/4 cup of oats (rolled)
*1/4 cup of bananas (chunked)
*7 strawberries (frozen)
*1/4 teaspoon of vanilla extract
*3/4 teaspoon of honey

Directions:

In a blender, add 1/2 cup of milk, 1/4 cup of oats (rolled), 1/4 cup of bananas (chunked), 7 strawberries (frozen), 1/4 teaspoon of vanilla extract, and 3/4 teaspoon of honey and blend until smooth. Pour into a glass and serve. Might want to serve with a spoon!

Pomegranate Smoothie

This is a refreshingly different fruit smoothie with pomegranates, mangoes and berries.

Makes 1 serving.

Ingredients:

*1/3 cup of milk
*1/4 cup of blueberries
*1/4 cup of raspberries
*1/4 cup of pomegranate juice
*1/4 cup of mango juice
*2 strawberries
*1 tablespoon of honey

Directions:

In a blender add 1/3 cup of milk, 1/4 cup of blueberries, 1/4 cup of raspberries, 1/4 cup of pomegranate juice, 1/4 cup of mango juice, 2 strawberries, and 1 tablespoon of honey and blend until smooth. Pour into a glass and enjoy. For a frosty smoothie freeze all the fruit first.

Melon Smoothie

This is a refreshing and thirst quenching smoothie.

Makes 1 serving.

Ingredients:

*1/2 cup of watermelon (no seeds, cubed)
*1/4 cup of honeydew melon (cubed)
*1/4 cup of milk
*2 tablespoons of ice cubes
*2 tablespoons of milk

Directions:

In a blender, add 1/2 cup of watermelon (no seeds, cubed), 1/4 cup of honeydew melon (cubed), 1/4 cup of milk, 2 tablespoons of ice cubes, and 2 tablespoons of milk and blend until smooth. Pour into a glass and enjoy.

Vegetable Smoothies (Also known as green smoothies)

Veggie Nut Smoothie

This is definitely a smoothie meant for lunch or supper.

Makes 1 serving.

Ingredients:

*3/4 cup of spinach
*1/2 cup of carrots (shredded)
*1/4 cup of beets (raw sliced)
*1/4 cup of milk
*1/4 cup of bananas (chunked)
*1/4 pear (no core, chopped)
*2 tablespoons of cottage cheese
*2 tablespoons of walnuts (chopped)
*2 tablespoons of almonds (chopped)
*1 tablespoon of yogurt (Greek)
*1 1/2 teaspoons of honey
*1/4 teaspoon of cinnamon (ground)

Directions:

In a blender add 3/4 cup of spinach, 1/2 cup of carrots (shredded), 1/4 cup of beets (raw sliced), 1/4 cup of milk, 1/4 cup of bananas (chunked), 1/4 pear (no core, chopped), 2 tablespoons of cottage cheese, 2 tablespoons of walnuts (chopped), 2 tablespoons of almonds (chopped), 1 tablespoon of yogurt (Greek), 1 1/2 teaspoons of honey, and 1/4 teaspoon of cinnamon (ground) and blend until smooth. Pour into a glass and enjoy.

Creamy Papaya Smoothie

A unique smoothie made with cream cheese.

Makes 1 serving.

Ingredients:

*1/3 cup papaya (peeled, seeded, chunked)
*1/3 cup of milk
*1/3 cup of ice
*2 1/4 tablespoons of yogurt (vanilla)
*2 teaspoons of honey
*2 teaspoons of sweetened condensed milk
*1 teaspoon of cream cheese

Directions:

In a blender add 1/3 cup papaya (peeled, seeded, chunked), 1/3 cup of milk, 1/3 cup of ice, 2 1/4 tablespoons of yogurt (vanilla), 2 teaspoons of honey, 2 teaspoons of sweetened condensed milk, and 1 teaspoon of cream cheese and blend until smooth. Pour in a glass and enjoy.

Strawberry Mud Smoothie

It is true, this smoothie looks like a glass of mud, but it tastes like sweet strawberry banana.

Makes 1 serving.

Ingredients:

*1/2 cup of spinach (frozen)
*1/2 cup of strawberries (frozen)
*1/4 cup of banana (chunked)
*2 tablespoons of ice
*1 1/2 teaspoon of honey

Directions:

In a blender, add 1/2 cup of spinach (frozen), 1/2 cup of strawberries (frozen), 1/4 cup of banana (chunked), 2 tablespoons of ice, and 1 1/2 teaspoon of honey and blend until smooth. Pour in a glass and enjoy. Really, it tastes better than it looks!

Zucchini Orange Smoothie

This beautiful light green colored smoothie tastes like delicious orange vanilla.

Makes 1 serving.

Ingredients:

*1/2 of a zucchini (cubed)
*3 ice cubes
*1/2 cup of orange juice
*1 tablespoon of honey
*1/4 teaspoon of vanilla extract

Directions:

In a blender, add 1/2 of a zucchini (cubed), 3 ice cubes, 1/2 cup of orange juice, 1 tablespoon of honey, and 1/4 teaspoon of vanilla extract and blend until smooth. Pour in a glass and enjoy.

Silly Sweet Zucchini Smoothie

It is silly sweet, because the only flavors you will taste in this smoothie are the bananas, cocoa and peanuts.

Makes 1 serving.

Ingredients:

*1/4 cup of zucchini (grated and frozen)
*1/4 cup of bananas (chunked)
*1/4 cup of half and half
*1/2 tablespoons of cocoa powder
*2 tablespoons of peanuts (finely chopped)
*1 tablespoon of honey

Directions:

In a blender add 1/4 cup of zucchini (grated and frozen), 1/4 cup of bananas (chunked), 1/4 cup of half and half, 1/2 tablespoons of cocoa powder, 2 tablespoons of peanuts (finely chopped), and 1 tablespoon of honey and blend until smooth. Pour into a glass and enjoy.

California Delight Smoothie

California is famous for their avocados and this smoothie is filled with them.

Makes 1 serving.

Ingredients:

*1/2 of an avocado (diced)
*1/4 cup of yogurt (vanilla)
*1/4 cup of milk
*1/8 cup of coconut cream
*4 ice cubes

Directions:

In a blender, add 1/2 of an avocado (diced), 1/4 cup of yogurt (vanilla), 1/4 cup of milk, 1/8 cup of coconut cream, and 4 ice cubes and blend until smooth. Pour in a glass and enjoy.

Pineapple Kiwi Smoothie

Not only will you taste pineapple and kiwi, but there is banana and the goodness of carrots in this smoothie.

Makes 1 serving.

Ingredients:

*1/2 cup of carrots (chopped)
*1/4 cup of banana (chopped)
*1/2 cup of apple (peeled, cored and chopped)
*1/2 cup of pineapple (chopped)
*1/2 cup of ice cubes
*1/4 cup of kiwi (peeled and chopped)

In a blender add: 1/2 cup of carrots (chopped), 1/4 cup of banana (chopped),1/2 cup of apple (peeled, cored and chopped), 1/2 cup of pineapple (chopped), 1/2 cup of ice cubes, and 1/4 cup of kiwi (peeled and chopped). Blend until smooth, pour into a glass, and enjoy.

Melon Cucumber Broccoli Smoothie

This smoothie turns into such a pretty shade of green, but tastes like fruit.

Makes 1 serving.

Ingredients:

*3/4 cup of honeydew melon (chunked)
*3/4 cup of ice cubes
*1/4 cup of grapes (green and seedless)
*1/4 cup of cucumber (no seeds and peeled)
*2 tablespoons of broccoli florets
*1/4 sprig of mint (fresh)

Directions:

In a blender add 3/4 cup of honeydew melon (chunked), 3/4 cup of ice cubes, 1/4 cup of grapes (green and seedless), 1/4 cup of cucumber (no seeds and peeled), 2 tablespoons of broccoli florets, and 1/4 sprig of mint (fresh) and blend until smooth. Pour in a glass and enjoy.

Truly Green Smoothie

Do not let the name fool you, it may be very green in color, but you will only taste the apples, pears, and cinnamon.

Makes 1 serving.

Ingredients:

*1/2 cup of apple juice
*1/2 cup of spinach
*1/3 cup of pears (chopped)
*1/3 cup of apples (chopped)
*1/2 teaspoon of cinnamon (ground)
*1/4 cup of ice

Directions:

Add the 1/2 cup of apple juice to a blender along with the 1/2 cup of spinach, 1/3 cup of chopped pears, 1/3 cup of chopped apples, 1/2 teaspoon of ground cinnamon, and the 1/4 cup of ice and blend until smooth. Pour in a glass and enjoy.

CocoCranNut Smoothie

This refreshing smoothie has way more than just coconut and cranberries, there are also avocados, cherries, blueberries and even basil. This is not your ordinary smoothie.

Makes 1 extra-large serving or 2 small servings.

Ingredients:

*1 cup of blueberries
*1 cup of yogurt (vanilla Greek)
*1/4 cup of cranberries (dried)
*1/4 cup of banana (chunked)
*1/2 avocado (pitted and chunked)
*10 cherries (pitted)
*5 cashews
*2 basil leaves (chopped)
*2 tablespoons of coconut flakes
*tablespoons of flax seeds (ground)
*1 teaspoon of chia seeds
*1 teaspoon of honey
*dash of cinnamon

Directions:

In the blender add 1 cup of blueberries, 1 cup of yogurt (vanilla Greek), 1/4 cup of cranberries (dried), 1/4 cup of banana (chunked), 1/2 avocado (pitted and chunked), 10 cherries (pitted), 5 cashews, 2 basil leaves (chopped), 2 tablespoons of coconut flakes, tablespoons of flax seeds (ground), 1 teaspoon of chia seeds, 1 teaspoon of honey, and a dash of cinnamon and blend until smooth. You may need to pulse at first to blend all the ingredients. Pour into a large glass or two small glasses and enjoy.

Gingered Veggie Fruit Smoothie

This smoothie is not only delicious but serves as a great supper substitute or for lunch.

Makes 1 serving.

Ingredients:

*2 cups of water (cold)
*1 avocado (peeled, pitted and chopped)
*1 apple (core removed and chopped)
*1 carrot (chunks)
*1 lemon (peeled and quartered)
*1 kale leaf
*1 piece of ginger root (1 inch)
*1/2 cup of parsley (fresh)
*1 tablespoon of flax seeds
*2 ice cubes

Directions:

First, pour the 2 cups of cold water into the blender and add the peeled, pitted and chopped avocado, cored and chopped apple, chunked carrot, peeled and quartered lemon, the kale leaf (rip it apart), the 1 inch ginger root (chopped), 1/2 cup of fresh parsley, tablespoon of flax seeds and blend until it reaches desired texture. Pour in a glass and enjoy.

Rhubarb Fruit Smoothie

Even though rhubarb is a vegetable, it is often used in desserts because of its sweet flavor.

Makes 1 serving.

Ingredients:

*1/2 cup of rhubarb (chopped and frozen)
*1/2 cup of cranberry juice
*1/4 cup of yogurt (vanilla)
*1/4 cup of banana (chunks)
*1 teaspoon of honey

Directions:

Add the 1/2 cup of chopped, frozen rhubarb, 1/2 cup of cranberry juice, 1/4 cup of vanilla yogurt, 1/4 cup of banana chunks and the teaspoon of honey into a blender and blend until it reaches desired consistency. Pour into a glass and enjoy.

Banana Chocolate Mint Green Smoothie

A delightful twist with a smoothie with the addition of chocolate and mint with the hidden goodness of spinach.

Makes 1 serving.

Ingredients:

*1/2 cup of spinach leaves
*1/4 cup of coconut milk (chilled)
*1/4 cup of banana (chopped frozen)
*1/8 cup of cocoa powder (unsweetened)
*5 mint leaves (fresh chopped)
*1/2 gram of stevia powder
*1/2 teaspoon of peppermint extract
*ice
*water

Directions:

In a blender add the 1/2 cup of spinach leaves, 1/4 cup of chilled coconut milk, 1/8 cup of unsweetened cocoa powder, 5 fresh chopped mint leaves, 1/2 gram of stevia powder, 1/2 teaspoon of peppermint extract. Blend until well mixed. Add the 1/4 cup of chopped frozen banana and blend. Add ice and or water and blend until desired consistency. Pour into a glass and enjoy.

Spicy Tomato Smoothie

Enjoy this savory vegetable infused smoothie.

Makes 1 serving.

Ingredients:

*1 cup of tomatoes (chopped)
*1 cup of ice
*1/4 cup of tomato juice
*1/4 cup of carrots (chopped)
*1/8 cup of celery (chopped)
*1/8 cup of apple juice
*dash of hot sauce

Directions:

In a blender, add the 1/4 cup of chopped carrots and 1/8 cup of chopped celery with the 1/8 cup of apple juice and blend until vegetables are pureed. Add the cup of chopped tomatoes, cup of ice and the 1/4 cup of tomato juice and blend along with the dash of hot sauce. Blend until it reaches desired consistency. Pour into glass and enjoy.

Broccoli Smoothie

Broccoli is one of the super foods therefore this is one healthy and tasty smoothie.

Makes 1 serving.

Ingredients:

*4 broccoli florets
*2 oranges (peeled)
*1 carrot (chopped)
*1 apple (cored and chopped)
*2 cups of spinach
*orange juice as needed

Directions:

First, you may want to juice the carrot and apple, if not, just chop them up into small chunks. Add the 4 broccoli florets, 2 oranges (quartered), chopped or juiced carrot and apple, 2 cups of spinach (loosely chopped) into a blender. Drizzle some orange juice and blend until it reaches desired consistency. Add more orange juice if needed. Pour into a glass and enjoy.

Orange Carrot Cantaloupe Smoothie

This is a refreshing smoothie with carrots, but all you taste is the delicious cantaloupe.

Makes 1 serving.

Ingredients:

*1 cup of cantaloupe (diced and ripe)
*1/2 cup of carrot juice
*1/2 cup of frozen yogurt (vanilla)
*1 tablespoon of orange juice (straight from the frozen concentrate can)

Directions:

Add the 1 cup of diced ripe cantaloupe, 1/2 cup of carrot juice, 1/2 cup of frozen vanilla yogurt and tablespoon of frozen orange juice concentrate to the blender and blend until smooth. Pour into glass and enjoy.

Avocado Maple Smoothie

This smoothie gives energy because it is a well-balanced drink.

Makes 1 serving.

Ingredients:

*1 avocado (peeled, pitted, cubed)
*1 cup of whey protein powder (vanilla)
*1/4 cup of ice
*1/4 cup of milk
*1/8 cup of sweetened condensed milk
*1/8 cup of maple syrup

Directions:

Add the peeled, pitted and cubed avocado to a blender along with the cup of vanilla whey protein powder, 1/4 cup of ice, 1/4 cup of milk, 1/8 cup of sweetened condensed milk and 1/8 cup of maple syrup. Blend until smooth and pour into glass to serve.

Spicy Vegetable Smoothie

This hot and savory smoothie is definitely not your typical breakfast smoothie; this is more for lunch or supper.

Makes 1 serving.

Ingredients:

*4 cups of celery (chopped)
*2 cups of tomatoes (chopped)
*2 red bell peppers (chopped)
*1 zucchini
*1/4 cup of onions (sliced)
*1/4 cup of avocado (chunked)
*1 tablespoon of chili powder
*1 teaspoon of flax seeds
*1/2 teaspoon of dulse flakes
*dash of cayenne pepper
*1 celery stalk

Directions:

First, add the 2 cups of chopped tomatoes in a blender and puree. Next, add the 2 chopped red bell peppers and the chopped zucchini and blend. Next, add the 4 cups of chopped celery, 1/4 cup of sliced onions, 1/4 cup of chunked avocado, tablespoon of chili powder, teaspoon of flax seeds, 1/2 teaspoon of dulse flakes and a dash of cayenne pepper. Pour into a tall glass, garnish with the stalk of celery, and enjoy.

Kale Smoothie

Here is a vegetable smoothie that will taste like cool grapes.

Makes 1 serving.

Ingredients:

*1 cup of grapes (green seedless)
*1 cup of kale
*1/2 cup of ice cubes

Directions:

Add the cups of green seedless grapes and kale in the blender along with the 1/2 cup of ice cubes. Blend until smooth, pour in a glass and enjoy.

Vanilla Yam Smoothie

Yams are naturally sweet and this makes this vegetable smoothie even sweeter.

Makes 1 serving.

Ingredients:

*1/4 of a yam (cooked)
*1/3 cup of yogurt (vanilla)
*1/4 cup of ice (crushed)
*1/4 cup of banana (chunked)
*1/8 cup of milk
*drizzle of honey (to taste)

Directions:

In a blender add 1/4 of a yam (cooked), 1/3 cup of yogurt (vanilla), 1/4 cup of ice (crushed), 1/4 cup of banana (chunked), 1/8 cup of milk, and then a drizzle of honey (to taste) and blend until smooth. Pour in a glass and enjoy.

Sweet Potato Banana Smoothie

Another naturally sweet vegetable smoothie this time using sweet potato.

Makes 1 serving.

Ingredients:

*1 cup of milk
*1/2 of a sweet potato (baked)
*1/4 cup of banana (chunked)
*1/8 teaspoon of cinnamon (ground)

Directions:

Prep: After baking the sweet potato, place in refrigerator for several hours or overnight to completely cool. Remove peel.

In a blender, add 1 cup of milk, 1/2 of a sweet potato (baked, peeled and cooled), 1/4 cup of banana (chunked), and 1/8 teaspoon of cinnamon (ground) and blend until smooth. Pour in a glass and enjoy.

Banana Kale Orange Smoothie

All you taste is the banana and orange in this delicious vegetable smoothie.

Makes 1 serving.

Ingredients:

*1 orange (peeled and quartered)
*1 kale leaf (torn into pieces)
*1/2 cup of water (cold)
*1 cup of bananas (chunked)

Directions:

First, add the orange in the blender and blend. Next, add the 1/2 cup of cold water and the kale leaf pieces and blend. Last, add the cup of banana chunks and blend until smooth. Smoothie will be thick. Pour in a glass and drink or spoon eat.

Eat Your Vegetables Smoothie

This smoothie has spinach and carrots, but you will taste the apples, orange, bananas and strawberries!
Makes 1 serving.

Ingredients:

*1/2 cup of spinach
*1/4 cup of bananas (chunked)
*1/4 cup of carrots (finely chopped)
*1/4 cup of orange juice
*1/4 cup of strawberries
*1/4 cup of ice
*half an apple (peeled, cored and chopped)

Directions:

In a blender add 1/2 cup of spinach, 1/4 cup of bananas (chunked), 1/4 cup of carrots (finely chopped), 1/4 cup of orange juice, 1/4 cup of strawberries, 1/4 cup of ice, and half an apple (peeled, cored and chopped) and blend until smooth. Pour in a glass and enjoy.

Tofu Smoothies

Chocolate Tofu Smoothie

A healthy smoothie with the favored flavor of chocolate combined with the healthy protein of tofu.

Makes 1 serving.

Ingredients:

*1/2 cup of milk
*1/4 cup of tofu (silken, chunked)
*1/4 cup of banana (chunks)
*1/3 tablespoon of honey
*2/3 tablespoon of chocolate drink mix
*1/8 tablespoon of wheat germ

Directions:

In a blender, add the 1/2 cup of milk, 1/4 cup of tofu (silken, chunked), 1/4 cup of banana (chunks), 1/3 tablespoon of honey, 2/3 tablespoon of chocolate drink mix, and 1/8 tablespoon of wheat germ and blend until smooth. Pour in a glass and enjoy.

Banana Berry Tofu Smoothie

The delicious combination of strawberries, blueberries and banana combined with protein rich tofu makes this a nutritious smoothie.

Makes 1 serving.

Ingredients:

*1/2 cup of yogurt (vanilla)
*1/2 cup of milk
*1/2 cup of strawberries
*1/3 cup of blueberries
*1/4 cup of banana
*1 1/2 inch cube of tofu (soft)

Directions:

Add the 1/2 cup of vanilla yogurt to a blender along with the 1/2 cup of milk, 1/4 cup of banana and the 1 1/2 inch cube of soft tofu, and blend until smooth. Add the 1/2 cup of strawberries and 1/3 cup of blueberries and blend again. Pour into a glass and enjoy.

Apple Strawberry Banana Smoothie

Protein rich smoothie with the flavor of apples, strawberries, and bananas.

Makes 1 serving.

Ingredients:

*1/2 cup of strawberries
*1/4 cup of apple juice
*1/4 cup of yogurt (frozen vanilla)
*1/4 cup of tofu (soft)
*1/4 cup of banana (chunked)
*1/4 cup of ice cubes
*1/2 tablespoon of honey
*1 strawberry (sliced)

In a blender add the 1/2 cup of strawberries, 1/4 cup of apple juice, 1/4 cup of frozen vanilla yogurt, 1/4 cup of soft tofu, 1/4 cup of chunked banana, 1/2 tablespoon of honey and blend until smooth. Add the 1/4 cup of ice cubes and blend until smooth. Pour into a glass, garnish with the sliced strawberries, and enjoy.

Apple Peach Banana Smoothie

Protein rich smoothie with the flavor of apples, peaches, and bananas.

Makes 1 serving.

Ingredients:

*1/2 cup of peaches (chunked)
*1/4 cup of apple juice
*1/4 cup of peach sorbet
*1/4 cup of tofu (soft)
*1/4 cup of banana (chunked)
*1/4 cup of ice cubes
*1/2 tablespoon of honey
*1 peach slice

In a blender add the 1/2 cup of strawberries, 1/4 cup of apple juice, 1/4 cup of peach sorbet, 1/4 cup of soft tofu, 1/4 cup of chunked banana, 1/2 tablespoon of honey and blend until smooth. Add the 1/4 cup of ice cubes and blend until smooth. Pour into a glass, garnish with the sliced peach, and enjoy.

Banana Raspberry Tofu Smoothie

Classic tofu makes a smoothie a complete meal replacement.

Makes 1 serving.

Ingredients:

*1/4 cup of tofu (silken)
*1/4 cup of milk
*1/4 cup of banana (chunked
*1/4 cup of raspberries
**2 tablespoons of orange juice (from frozen concentrate can)

Directions:

In a blender, add 1/4 cup of tofu (silken), 1/4 cup of milk, 1/4 cup of banana (chunked), 1/4 cup of raspberries, and 2 tablespoons of orange juice (from frozen concentrate can) and blend until smooth. Pour into a glass and enjoy.

5 Day Sample Menu

The smoothie diet is a diet in which these smoothie recipes are meant to replace an entire meal. This helps in two ways, first to facilitate weight loss, and second to reduce hunger. If you are counting calories, you can adjust the ingredients to accommodate more or less caloric intake. For example, use low fat or skim milk instead of 2% or whole milk. Use low fat yogurt, or light soymilk. Adjust according to your dieting needs.

Most of the smoothies in this book have protein in the form of a dairy product, soy, tofu, or even added protein powder. A few do not and those should be used as snacks or desserts only and not a full meal replacement. When preparing smoothies, most are best consumed immediately. A few may last a day or two if stored in the refrigerator, especially those with no frozen ingredients. Fruit juice smoothies may last several days whereas dairy foods will make them less able to last longer than a day or two.

If you follow the smoothie diet, eating all the meals including the snacks, the hunger should stay away. If you skip any of the suggested meals, you will become hungry and a smoothie alone may not satisfy you. The goal is to make the stomach think it is full at all times. Smoothies are a healthy way to receive the vitamins and minerals contains in fruits and vegetables. For many people it is a very easy diet to follow and stick with and experience successful weight loss.

Day One

Breakfast
Peanut Banana Berry Smoothie

Mid Morning Snack
An apple

Lunch
Apple Strawberry Banana Smoothie

Mid-Afternoon Snack
Grapefruit half

Supper
Avocado Maple Smoothie

Day Two

Breakfast
Fruit Spread Smoothie

Mid Morning Snack
An orange

Lunch
Kale Smoothie

Mid-Afternoon Snack
Small bunch of grapes

Supper
A whole food plate of vegetables and one lean serving of meat

Day Three

Breakfast
Creamy Strawberry Smoothie

Mid Morning Snack
Glass of all-natural fruit punch

Lunch
Apple Peach Banana Smoothie

Mid-Afternoon Snack
Sliced Kiwi

Supper
Orange Carrot Cantaloupe Smoothie

Day Four

Breakfast
Refreshing Smoothie

Mid Morning Snack
A small bunch of grapes

Lunch
Spicy Vegetable Smoothie

Mid-Afternoon Snack
An apple

Supper
A whole food plate of vegetables and one lean serving of meat

Day Five

Breakfast
Peachy Banana Berry Smoothie

Mid Morning Snack
A grapefruit half

Lunch
Banana Berry Tofu Smoothie

Mid-Afternoon Snack
All-natural fruit punch

Supper
Broccoli Smoothie

This sample menu has a choice of a whole foods supper every other day. If you are too hungry and need more solid food, make every night a whole food supper. Or the opposite, if you can handle all smoothies all day, then go ahead and do that. This diet will help to lose weight and doing an all smoothie all day will help it to happen faster.

Printed in Great Britain
by Amazon.co.uk, Ltd.,
Marston Gate.